D1562554

Double Trouble in Recovery

Double Trouble in Recovery

BASIC GUIDE

HAZELDEN®

Hazelden
Center City, Minnesota 55012
hazelden.org

First published by DTR, Inc., 2000
First published by Hazelden, 2010. All rights reserved
Printed in the United States of America

Library of Congress Cataloging-in-Publication Data
Double Trouble in Recovery : basic guide.
p. cm.
ISBN 978-1-59285-829-3 (softcover)
1. Dual diagnosis—Patients—Rehabilitation. 2. Twelve-step programs.
I. Double Trouble in Recovery (Group)
RC564.68.D686 2010
362.29—dc22
2009054134

Editor's note
The publication of this work does not imply, nor does it suggest, any affiliation with, nor approval of
or endorsement from Alcoholics Anonymous World Services, Inc., or any other Twelve Step Fellowship
patterned after Alcoholics Anonymous. All quotations from the book *Alcoholics Anonymous* can be found
in the fourth edition of that book.

All quotes from *Twelve Steps and Twelve Traditions*, a copyrighted publication of Alcoholics Anonymous
World Services, Inc., are used with permission. Alcoholics Anonymous is a registered trademark of
Alcoholics Anonymous World Services, Inc.

The Twelve Steps and Twelve Traditions of Alcoholics Anonymous have been adapted by Double
Trouble in Recovery (DTR) and are used with permission.

In publishing this work we in no way intend to give mental health advice or advice on medications.
We do not offer or imply mental health treatment to anyone or claim a cure of any kind. If you have a
mental health and/or addiction problem, always seek the advice of a qualified mental health professional
before making any decisions. This publication is for educational purposes only and not for planning
your own treatment for mental health problems and/or addictions.

14 13 12   2 3 4 5 6

Cover design by David Spohn
Interior design and typesetting by Ryan Scheife, Mayfly Design

Contents

Preface

Double Trouble in Recovery (DTR) is a fellowship of men and women who share their experience, strength, and hope with each other so that they may solve their common problems and help others recover from their particular addictions and manage their mental disorders. DTR is designed to meet the needs of people who, in addition to having a substance abuse problem, have also been diagnosed with a mental disorder (this is often called a "dual diagnosis"). For many of us, having addiction and mental disorders represents "double trouble in recovery"—trouble that is often further complicated by the problems and benefits of psychiatric medications.

Adapted from the Twelve Step program of Alcoholics Anonymous, the DTR fellowship is founded upon equality, one dually diagnosed person sharing and talking with, and never down to, another. Like AA and other such groups, the DTR program is built around regular meetings, a sponsorship system, and mutual support in "working the Steps" and adhering to the program's "Traditions." The only requirement for membership is a desire to stop drinking and drugging and to work on one's mental health. Members pay no dues or fees; we are self-supporting through our own contributions.

Many of us with substance abuse problems and mental disorders have followed the Steps and Traditions of other mutual support programs that address either alcoholism or drug addiction. We needed a program that addressed both substance addictions *and* mental disorders. Established in 1989, DTR has now grown to the point where we can set down on paper our own Steps and Traditions. This book, written in the collective voice of those in DTR, is the result.

Introduction

Do you have double trouble? If you are dually diagnosed with a mental disorder as well as a substance use problem, this book is for you. It can help you along the Twelve Step path to recovery, to a new life. This guide is meant to serve as a basic text for the Double Trouble in Recovery fellowship, just as the "Big Book," officially titled *Alcoholics Anonymous*, is the basic text of AA.

In fact, the Big Book is so useful that this guide comments on it and quotes from it often. You'll also see references to another book, *Twelve Steps and Twelve Traditions*. This guide can be read with or without those books at hand, and with or without belonging to a DTR group, although joining one is highly recommended.

While the Big Book focuses on alcoholism, its principles apply to any kind of substance dependence. You don't have to be an alcoholic to use the practical wisdom in the Big Book. Give it a chance, and give yourself a chance. As you read this *Double Trouble in Recovery Basic Guide*, it will become clear that the struggles we face—with drugs, alcohol, or both—are similar to those described in the Big Book. And, while our struggles with mental disorders are somewhat different, the solution and the Twelve Step program of action are the same.

We thank the AA program and its founders as we follow in their footsteps. We also thank all the DTR members who collaborated on this book. We are not experts, but individuals who have learned a few things in our recoveries and have a desire to share them with other dually diagnosed individuals. "You have to give it away to keep it," as the program wisdom has it. We are in recovery from mental disorders and substance abuse, and we know how hard it is to apply the Twelve Steps to our lives. This book brings together a collection of our experiences with dual diagnosis and with recovery using the Twelve Step program as detailed in the Big Book. This is not a philosophy; this is a living program, to be believed and lived to the best of our abilities. We share what we know and we strive toward progress, not perfection. We don't speak officially for DTR or for any other Twelve Step program as a whole. Feel free to argue or to disagree with anything you read in this commentary; no matter what, don't let it turn you away from the program.

In writing this commentary, we hope to help our brothers and sisters—and ourselves—attain happiness and freedom from our addictions and from mental disorders. It's a great honor to share what we know about dual diagnosis and how the Twelve Steps of DTR apply to our path of recovery. We have striven to keep open minds and to honestly expose our problems and weaknesses. But the humility we show shall never mask the courage it takes to admit who and what we are, as together we find the hope and strength that gradually broaden our narrow path into a wide road leading to peace, serenity, and a meaningful life.

Our fellowship is about one dually diagnosed human being helping another. It's true that those of us in recovery are sometimes closed-minded, and thus we sometimes find following our spiritual teaching difficult, for none of us really wants to find out too much about ourselves. But we have nonetheless seen tolerance expressed to us in a variety of ways in DTR: in kindness and consideration toward the newcomer just starting on the path of recovery; in understanding those who perhaps have been less fortunate; and in empathy toward those whose ideas may seem to differ greatly from our own. These spiritual principles are crucial. Without them, we doubt that the type of giving we offer each other could keep anybody clean, sober, and out of the hospital. With them, we can talk about our problems and suggest a solution and a practical program of action. In this book we explain how this program emerges from our experiences, our truth. Together, by sharing these experiences, we can learn to help each other.

Few of us come to the Double Trouble in Recovery program beaming with hope, faith, and understanding. If you are reading this book, you might doubt that the DTR program can work for you. Many of us had such doubts. We urge you to read on a little further, however, because you may find that we are telling your story as well as our own. Maybe you, too, can have a new experience by following this program. DTR is a practical program that we "work" in our daily lives by taking specific actions.

As dually diagnosed people, we can use the Twelve Steps to address not only our substance dependence but our mental disorders as well. This book addresses not only substance issues but also the stigma of mental illness and the challenge of managing a mental disorder. We search for a spiritual solution for our troubles, for acceptance of our mental disorder without the stigma, and for identification with our fellows.

If you can find (or start) a DTR group in your area, you can meet regularly with other dually diagnosed people: people who may have much in common with you, people who can share support, ideas, and fellowship. Like other Twelve Step meetings, these generally are held at least weekly. They offer mutual support, sharing of experiences, and a sponsorship system that partners newcomers with others further along the recovery path. Check the Web site www.double troubleinrecovery.org for more information.

We recommend attending other Twelve Step meetings as well: Alcoholics Anonymous, Narcotics Anonymous, Dual Recovery Anonymous, and many other groups have developed a nationwide meeting network for those with substance use problems. Check the Internet or your local telephone directory.

As dually diagnosed people, we suffer physically, emotionally, mentally, and spiritually. We have physical cravings and mental obsessions and find ourselves powerless over them. Those of us in the DTR fellowship found that we needed to have a vital spiritual experience to recover. By understanding the problem, seeing the solution, and applying the program of action, we hope you will have the vital experience necessary to start you on the path to recovery. We hope you will decide to join us. All that's needed is a beginning. In the words of the Big Book (page 568), "Willingness, honesty and open mindedness are the essentials of recovery. But these are indispensable."

While we refer often to the Big Book, remember, this guide can be used alone. It has been organized to include everything you need to get started and to work on our program of recovery. In the chapters that follow, you can read in detail about Steps One through Twelve. These chapters may be read alone, with a sponsor, or aloud during a meeting. Each chapter ends with relevant quotes from the Big Book or *Twelve Steps and Twelve Traditions* (also known as the "Twelve and Twelve") and a short list of questions to help you get the most out of each Step. The book also includes a description of each of the Twelve Traditions: tried-and-true principles that help recovery groups function at their best.

As with all textbooks, this one should be read in order, from beginning to end, as each section builds on the last. Used in that way, this guide gives us a set of tools to use in our recovery process. Before you start doing the work suggested in this text, you may find it helpful to read it all the way through once, especially if you are new to the process of Twelve Step recovery.

This book is written in the spirit of AA's Twelve Steps, to carry a message to members of DTR and those who might join us. Many of us walked into our program not believing in anything. Without faith or hope we entered a DTR meeting room with closed minds, with little understanding of ourselves. But something drove us there—we were ready to face the fact that conducting our lives by self-will is what got us into trouble. You will learn that a life run on self-will cannot be a healthy life. You will learn to open yourself to a new experience, to put aside old ideas as we submit together to the Steps of recovery. This isn't always a comfortable process. But we need to have a new experience, because our old way of thinking is a liability and not an asset. This work is about sharing our lives. This guide is a tool to do that work. It will help us develop a living program and trust in a Higher Power. It will help us have a new experience with this power and will show us how to relate to our fellows. (*Note:* Many of us call this power "God." Although we use the word *He* in this book to refer to this "God of our understanding," we don't exclude anyone's conception of a Higher Power.)

This work is about treating a spiritual malady and learning to make progress, to be less alone, less afraid, and less empty, and to welcome positive change in our lives.

This book carries the message that we can recover from the seemingly hopeless state of mind, body, and spirit, and it shows how some of us have recovered. We are sharing not so much our knowledge but our experience with a way of living and its results. As the basic text of Double Trouble in Recovery, this book suggests a planned program of action to recover from our addictions and manage our mental disorders. We will learn to help each other recover from dual diagnosis, to stay spiritually fit one day at a time, and to share these tools with others. But just joining the fellowship, going to meetings, is not enough. We must carry the message to others and practice the principles of the program. We can all have a new experience and, in doing the work suggested here, recover from our spiritual malady—body, mind, and spirit.

We hope to meet you along the path.

The Twelve Steps of Double Trouble in Recovery

1. We admitted we were powerless over our mental disorders and substance abuse—that our lives had become unmanageable.
2. Came to believe that a Power greater than ourselves could restore us to sanity.
3. Made a decision to turn our will and our lives over to the care of God *as we understood Him.*
4. Made a searching and fearless moral inventory of ourselves.
5. Admitted to God, to ourselves, and to another human being the exact nature of our wrongs.
6. Were entirely ready to have God remove all these defects of character.
7. Humbly asked Him to remove our shortcomings.
8. Made a list of all persons we had harmed, and became willing to make amends to them all.

9. Made direct amends to such people wherever possible, except when to do so would injure them or others.

10. Continued to take personal inventory and when we were wrong promptly admitted it.

11. Sought through prayer and meditation to improve our conscious contact with God *as we understood Him*, praying only for knowledge of His will for us and the power to carry that out.

12. Having had a spiritual awakening as the result of these Steps, we tried to carry this message to other dually diagnosed people, and to practice these principles in all our affairs.

The Twelve Principles of
Double Trouble in Recovery

As you "work the Steps" of recovery, you'll see that each one is rooted in a principle, a guiding theme. Keep them in mind as you read. These are the building blocks of a healthy life.

Step 1 . . . . Honesty

Step 2 . . . . Hope

Step 3 . . . . Faith

Step 4 . . . . Courage

Step 5 . . . . Trust, Integrity

Step 6 . . . . Willingness

Step 7 . . . . Humility

Step 8 . . . . Forgiveness, Brotherly Love

Step 9 . . . . Restitution, Justice

Step 10 . . . . Perseverance

Step 11 . . . . Spirituality, Awareness

Step 12 . . . . Service

Step One

We admitted we were powerless over our mental disorders and substance abuse—that our lives had become unmanageable.

We are powerless over our mental disorders. We are powerless over our addictions. Before we admitted these truths, our lives were unmanageable. We were unable to handle life without drugs and alcohol or to take care of our mental health. We thought that drugs and alcohol would make us feel better. They did, at first. But those substances became our masters, and we lost control. Today, we truly accept the fact that we are addicts and alcoholics with a mental disorder. We accept both diagnoses. When it comes to our dual diagnosis, we are powerless.

Honesty with ourselves is central to Step One. As we review our past, we see that we cheated, stole, lied, and manipulated; we were dishonest, self-centered, self-seeking, inconsiderate, and frightened. We lived in opposition to truth and honesty, and we got caught. We suffered from drugs and alcohol. We tortured ourselves with barbiturates, cocaine, heroin, LSD, ice, crack, pills, and other mood-altering chemicals. We discovered that our bodies—our physical cravings—were as abnormal as our minds—our mental obsessions. Knowing we were out of control and could not tolerate drugs and alcohol didn't help. They were not our substances of "choice" but of "no-choice." We were sick, in full flight from reality, suffering mentally, physically, and spiritually.

For those of us in Double Trouble, it is rare that our alcoholism or other addiction can be permanently cured by any treatment. But although it may be incurable, it is treatable. How? Through absolute abstinence from our "substance of no-choice." The stakes could not be higher. Our addiction cost us almost everything worthwhile in life. We lived without hope. We hated ourselves and our own diagnosis. We decided our situation was hopeless. We often used drugs or alcohol to mask our mental and emotional symptoms. Some of us were lonely, without family or friends, and with no one wanting to know us. People turned away from us. Our drinking or drugging was no longer a comfort or a luxury. It was a necessity become a routine. We told ourselves that one day we would quit—but always tomorrow, not today. And tomorrow didn't come right away. In fact, it didn't come for years.

Drinking and drugging frequently made our mental disorder symptoms worse. No words can describe the torture we felt, shuttling in and out of hospitals and institutions, sometimes homeless, overcome with despair and self-pity. Drugs, alcohol, and our symptoms were our masters. Only when hospitalized did we stop using—until we were released to the streets to start in again. We were so powerless, but we somehow still thought we were powerful. In the First Step of our recovery, we must admit defeat. Until we can do that, our lives will remain unmanageable.

Let's look more closely at our first diagnosis: addiction. At some stage of our drinking or drugging career we reached a point where, as soon as we started, we would lose control over the amount we would use. Craving became sufficient reason in and of itself to keep using. We were both physically and mentally impaired. Some of us could drink and stop but not drug and stop, or vice versa. The issue is control: Have we lost control? Are we powerless over our substance use? (See "On substance dependence" at the end of this chapter.) The disease of addiction is not something we make up our own minds about. We drank and drugged no matter what, not because we could stop when we wanted to, but because we couldn't stop. That aspect of our experience reveals a key truth. As you consider the First Step, ask yourself this question: once you put alcohol or drugs in your system, does it seem virtually impossible for you to stop? Accepting that fact is key: once the substance is in our system, we lose control and can't stop.

Again, as addicts and alcoholics, we are sick in body and in mind. Craving and compulsion control our bodies; addiction controls our minds. The tricks it plays on the mind include denial, rationalization, and other mental defense mechanisms. Remember: addiction is a disease that tells us that we don't have it. And even if we admit our problem after years of denial, we may find ourselves unable to stop.

The process of addiction may be a gradual one. Over time, we find that we've built a tolerance to the addictive substance: we need more of it to get the same effect. Not only that, we've become dependent on it. Before we knew it, we needed a drink to socialize or a joint to relax. So we tried not to use. We tried the geographical cure, physically moving away from our problems. We stayed away from the people, places, and things that we associated with our out-of-control behavior. But our minds continued to play tricks on us. They told us that free of outside influences, we could now control our drinking or drugging. We could use just one time. This is the obsession of the mind. We trusted our mind, and we used. Then our bodies reacted to the alcohol or the drug, and, having started, we couldn't stop. We became symptomatic and ended up in the hospital. This is how the vicious cycle of using begins again and again, and we can't stop it, even if we tell ourselves to stop. We are caught in the cycle of addiction, and we have no freedom. Our actions prove our addiction by how we live to use and use to live. Our obsessive thinking about using every day, day in and day out, is equaled only by our physical cravings. We come to DTR because we realize that our own power alone can't help us do what has to be done to save our lives. Insight and self-understanding—knowing we have a problem—is valuable, but it's not enough.

Now let's look at the second part of our dual diagnosis. We ask ourselves, is our struggle with addiction compounded by a mental disorder? And how do we know if we have a mental disorder? One way is to be professionally diagnosed with schizophrenia, bipolar disorder, major depression, or any diagnosis describing psychotic thinking. Another way we may find that we have a mental disorder is by assessing our daily lives. Does our way of thinking or feeling get us into so much trouble that sometimes we can't live even a minimally satisfying life? Do our minds or emotions interfere with our daily functioning to such an extent that we can't make it through the day without major difficulties, even if we are clean and sober? If the answer is yes, then it's likely that we have a mental disorder. Perhaps at first we are unsure. If you're uncertain, pay extra attention to your gut. In your gut, not in your head, ask yourself for a conscious awareness of whether both of these diagnoses apply to you. Let *your* experience show you your truth. Don't go by anyone else's experience. Ask yourself: once I stop using, can I keep myself stopped? For most of us, the answer will be no. We ask ourselves these questions so that we might find our own truth.

Especially with regard to mental health, it's wise to seek a professional opinion. But we must fully "own" our diagnosis ourselves. If you're told you have a mental disorder, take it seriously. Does it match with your own experience? Define yourself by your own experience. Find out your own truth. The mind will lie—about its own health, and about its addictions. But your experience will not lie to you if you let it speak for itself. Let no one tell you whether or not you are a drug addict or an alcoholic or both. Listen, then search your own life for the evidence. Make it your own opinion. Listen to your experience and ask yourself: Am I physically powerless over alcohol and drugs? Do I have a mental disorder?

We become honest by discovering our own truth. Understanding comes, but only slowly, through awareness and acceptance of conditions *as they are*. We know we have problems, but the truth is hard to accept. In order to recover, however, the truth *must* be accepted. We come to know this as a fact in our recovery. Admitting powerlessness is not a sign of weakness. It simply means that when it comes to substance use and to struggling with mental disorders, we are not in charge. Willpower has no meaning when it comes to controlling our use of drugs and alcohol and our mental processes. Before we took the First Step, we had a distorted view of ourselves and of our lives, of what was real and what was not. The First Step can set us free. Not just reading or reciting it, but living it through experience. Our whole recovery rests on the First Step premise.

We shall continually return to this principle: Honesty sets you free. Once we accept our powerlessness, many of us experience the miracle of being freed from active addiction and from the obsession to use again. This is the paradox of recovery: that in accepting our powerlessness, we become empowered to stop using and to work on our mental disorders. This comes as a great relief. With recognition and acceptance, we are free. We never need to go back to drugs and alcohol again. Instead of being filled with our addictive thoughts of self-destruction, remorse, despair, rage, and sadness about our past, we look with great joy and comfort at these precious moments we are now given. Admitting complete defeat is not what we wanted, but it is what we needed. One part of us sincerely wanted to be free. Another part continued to want to drink and drug. We came to know that our addiction was greater than our will. It was a monster with an insatiable appetite, and we let it take from us all our self-sufficiency and our will to resist its demands.

If you still think you can handle that monster, try this simple test: Go ahead and stop, and stay stopped. Do without. If you are successful, there is no addiction. But if you cannot stop and stay stopped, no amount of willpower or denial will change the fact that you are addicted. In regard to whether you have a mental disorder, try this: If you are manic, slow down. If you hear voices, stop them. If you are depressed, feel better. If you cannot, you have a mental disorder.

This program won't be easy at first. When our bodies are deprived of something they have been accustomed to, they respond with danger signals: uneasiness, irritability, extreme agitation or panic, rapid pulse, tremors. We become more aware of our mental health symptoms or our disease. Our bodies and our minds are telling us something is wrong. And now we know that something is wrong indeed. We are powerless over our addiction and mental disorders. Our lives have become unmanageable.

Having admitted this and having faced, perhaps for the first time, the mess our lives have become due to this spiritual malady, we come to see that if powerlessness is our problem, empowerment is the solution.

Relevant Quotes for Step One

On acceptance: In part 2 of the Big Book, AA members recount their own recovery experiences. In story 16, "Acceptance Was the Answer," the author writes, "Acceptance is the answer to *all* my problems today. When I am disturbed, it is because I find some person, place, thing, or situation—some fact of my life—unacceptable to me, and I can find no serenity until I accept that person, place, thing, or situation as being exactly the way it is supposed to be at this moment. Nothing, absolutely nothing happens in God's world by mistake. Until I accepted my alcoholism I couldn't stay sober; unless I accept life completely on life's terms, I cannot be happy. I need to concentrate not so much on what needs to be changed in the world, as on what needs to be changed in me and in my attitudes.

"Shakespeare said, 'All the world's a stage, and all the men and women merely players.' He forgot to mention that I was the chief critic. I was always able to see the flaw in every person, every situation. And I was always glad to point it out, because I knew you wanted perfection, just as I did. AA and acceptance have taught me that there is a bit of good in the worst of us and a bit of bad in the best of us; that we are all children of God and we each have a right to be here. When I complain about me or about you I am complaining about God's handiwork. I am saying that I know better than God." (Big Book, p. 417)

On powerlessness: In this absurd yet apt analogy, a compulsive jaywalker illustrates our own mental obsessions and our powerlessness in the face of drugs or alcohol: "He tries every known means to get the jaywalking idea out of his head. He shuts himself up in an asylum, hoping to mend his ways. But the day he comes out he races in front of a fire engine, which breaks his back. Such a man would be crazy, wouldn't he?" (Big Book, p. 38)

"Once more: The alcoholic at certain times has no effective mental defense against the first drink. Except in a few rare cases, neither he nor any other human being can provide such a defense. His defense must come from a Higher Power." (Big Book, p. 43)

On substance dependence: In the Big Book chapter titled "The Doctor's Opinion," William D. Silkworth, M.D., writes, "I do not hold with those who believe that alcoholism is entirely a problem of mental control . . . These men were not drinking to escape; they were drinking to overcome a craving beyond their mental control . . . They are over-remorseful and make many resolutions, but never a decision . . . There is the type who always believes that after being entirely free from alcohol for a period of time he can take a drink without danger . . . They cannot start drinking without developing the phenomena of craving . . . The only relief we have to suggest is entire abstinence." (Big Book, pp. xxix–xxx)

In chapter 4, the authors note, "If, when you honestly want to, you find you cannot quit entirely, or if when drinking, you have little control over the amount you take, you are probably alcoholic. If that be the case, you may be suffering from an illness which only a spiritual experience will conquer." (Big Book, p. 44)

Suggested Questions for Step One

1. In what ways are you powerless over drugs or alcohol?
2. In what ways are you struggling with having a mental disorder?

3. How has your life been unmanageable as a result of using drugs or alcohol?

4. How has your life been unmanageable as a result of struggling with a mental disorder?

Step Two

Came to believe that a Power greater than ourselves could restore us to sanity.

The end of drug and alcohol use is actually just the beginning. In Step One we prepare ourselves for the adventure of a new life by becoming honest and willing. In Step Two, we open our minds and our hearts and begin to believe in and find hope in a Power greater than our own. Nothing more is required of us. The willingness to believe is the starting point. There is no demand that you believe, and you don't have to take on all of Step Two right now. Step Two opens a door; it says that we "came to believe," not that we "came in believing." For most of us, belief and faith come gradually, as we start practicing the program and see it work for others like us. Easy does it.

The Steps are made to be used, not just discussed. We could sit and talk about hope, faith, courage and surrender, acceptance, honesty, humility, and gratitude—all of which are threads of the spiritual principles interwoven throughout the DTR program. But just talking about these things will not do it for us. Only when we apply the Twelve Step principles to our everyday problems and see them work do we begin to discover what sanity is. It is soundness and health of mind. When we are sane, we don't obsess about using, and we don't get hooked on mania or other "interesting" altered states.

At first, perhaps we can only grasp the Steps intellectually. With time, we start to believe in these principles. Then gradually we begin to live them, and we begin to experience a spiritual awakening. Old ideas, emotions, and attitudes are cast aside, and new ones replace them. To acquire these principles, we had only to stop fighting.

For some of us, faith in the "God idea" can be a real stumbling block. Before we entered recovery, many of us always prided ourselves on not needing anything or anybody. We were all-powerful and indestructible. Who needs God, right? Faith is for the constitutionally weak, those who can't make it on their own. Yet even in our addicted state, our lives rested on faith and on untested beliefs. Not faith in God, for sure—it was blind faith in our own invincibility. We believed we were masters of the universe when we drank or got high. As we were dying of our spiritual malady, we clung to the belief that we were indestructible, that drugs could and would help, that we didn't need our prescribed medication, that we knew better than anyone. So all along, we lived on beliefs and on faith.

Now, at the bottom, having admitted our powerlessness and unmanageability in Step One, it is time to consider that there may be a Power greater than ourselves. All that is needed to begin is willingness and an open mind. Many of us couldn't swallow the God idea, yet we knew that we could no longer rely on our own self-will. Our old ideas wouldn't work for us anymore. We needed to make a change physically, mentally, emotionally, and spiritually—we needed a new idea—and something inside us wanted to connect to this new idea. But we were helpless and hopeless. We needed to ask for help, but first we had to admit to ourselves that we needed help. We saw healthier ways of living and acting; we saw that members of our fellowship were willing to follow a simple set of principles and tools. Honesty, willingness, and open-mindedness were primary among them. They are the essentials of recovery. And they are indispensable.

For many of us, when we hear the word *God*, we think of our childhood concept of God, and we are completely turned off. But let us consider Ebby's words to Bill W., cofounder of Alcoholics Anonymous (quoted in the Big Book, page 12): "Why don't you choose your own conception of God[?]" Well, why not? Everything else has failed. Why not ask yourself this question: if you could pick the kind of God that you could believe in, what would He be like?

We know that you're risking quite a bit by trying to choose a God of your understanding. It is difficult and a

little scary at first. Some of us find we can base our conception of God on the acronym Good Orderly Direction. Or
we can imagine God as a friend, one who is never too busy to
listen to us, to our problems, our joys. Perhaps this new God
of our understanding will help us live another day, give us
the courage to face what we can't face alone, help us conquer
our fears. Perhaps He is patient, wise, and tolerant. To make
a beginning, we can conceive of our Higher Power as the
DTR fellowship itself, not just the members we know but
all our brothers and sisters everywhere who share a concern
for each other and, in doing so, create a spiritual resource
stronger than any one of us alone could provide.

When we use the term *God*, it is meant to refer to our
own individual conceptions of God. Don't let the word turn
you off. Rather, explore for what it means for *you*. That's all
you need to initiate spiritual growth. Do you now believe, or
are you now *willing* to believe, that there is a Power greater
than you are? You'll discover that God makes it easy for us to
approach Him; He is always available to those who earnestly
seek His help.

After looking at the powerlessness and unmanageability
of our lives in Step One, we came to see that a Power greater
than ourselves could and would help us. We had no trouble
believing that such a power *could* help us, but we had doubts
about whether He *would*. Mental disorders seemed so unjust
to us. Why me? Why anybody? We were deeply angry at
our Higher Power. If He allowed something that unfair to

happen to us, why would He do anything for us? We felt worthless. We were labeled by society as mentally ill. Why should God care? Why should anyone care? Our own pain became so great that in spite of ourselves, we honestly cried out for help. And in that cry of pain, we somehow knew that a Higher Power *would* help us. We came to believe.

The beauty of the Twelve Step program is that it is spiritual in nature, but not bound by the kind of theological doctrines that have caused harm to many of us. DTR is not a religious program. We see our powerlessness over our afflictions and addictions as a spiritual problem, the solution being to rely on a Power greater than ourselves, a power beyond our physical and mental capabilities. This doesn't happen overnight. Many of us didn't get over the craving for drugs and alcohol right away. Freeing ourselves from the obsession of the mind is a spiritual process. And a major part of that process is learning to accept ourselves as dually diagnosed people. To admit our dual diagnosis is to admit to ourselves our essential humanity. This isn't easy. But we learn from the fellowship that if others can accept us and love us as we are, then we can love ourselves for who we are and what we can become.

For those new to DTR, allow the fellowship to accept you until you can accept yourself. When we say, "Hi, my name is _____, and I am dually diagnosed," we are saying, "I am a human being, and I have worth." This admission grants each of us the awareness that "I am a human being and there is hope for my recovery." It also gives us the opportunity to learn more about humanity by learning about ourselves. This is the beginning of a new way of living and thinking.

We in DTR believe that the vital spiritual experience we have in the fellowship has brought us the extraordinary gift of sanity and sobriety, which in turn is what gives value to our lives. For a substance abuser with a mental disorder, the decision to live on a spiritual basis is not an easy one to make. But through the strength we receive from the fellowship, we found that we could accept who we are and then come to believe that a Power greater than ourselves could actually restore us to sanity. We learned that while our human capabilities were not sufficient to do so, God could, and would, if He were sought.

Our Higher Power did for us what we couldn't do for ourselves. The craving, obsession, and compulsion have left us. We have entered a new dimension of freedom under God as we understand Him. There is a relationship here. When we entered the program, our motivation to seek recovery was driven by the stigmas, hurt, shame, and guilt we'd experienced—combined with the grace of God, whether we realized it or not at the time. Surrender does not come easy for any dually diagnosed person, but in asking daily for His help, we learned humility. We were lost, no longer able to rely on our own resources. We found there is only one source. With time, we discarded our old lives and beliefs, the ones that did not work, for a new life, one that works under any condition. God's grace overcame our malady. That truth has set us free to regard ourselves as we regard any other person—as acceptable, for our Higher Power accepts us for what we are, imperfect human beings.

We don't like admitting that we can't handle drugs and alcohol and that we can't always control our moods and feelings. And although we know how these substances damaged our minds and bodies, a voice calling out from within us still wants us to use. So we accept the power drugs and alcohol have when we let them into our bodies. We see now that we were irrational. We put drugs and alcohol before everything else. In admitting our powerlessness, we identified the problem; in coming to believe in a Higher Power, we began to see the solution. We can live each day in the sunlight of the spirit, not in the darkness of addiction, seeking a Power greater than ourselves, a Power that can and will show us grace. Every day we renew our contract with ourselves through our Higher Power. Each morning we thank our Higher Power for a new beginning, a new day clean and sober and sane. The power of addiction can be broken. The shift is in coming to believe, and the proper response is to say to our Higher Power, "Thank you." Such an easy prayer that fills us with gratitude for what He has given us! We are now ready for Step Three.

Relevant Quotes for Step Two

On willingness: "Almost none of us liked the self-searching, the leveling of our pride, the confession of shortcomings . . . But we saw that it really worked in others, and we had come to believe in the hopelessness and futility of life as we had been living it. When, therefore, we were approached by those in whom the problem had been solved, there was nothing left for us but to pick up the simple kit of spiritual tools laid at our feet." (Big Book, p. 25)

"Is not our [era] characterized by the ease with which we discard old ideas for new, by the complete readiness with which we throw away the theory or gadget which does not work for something new which does?

"We had to ask ourselves why we shouldn't apply to our human problems the same readiness to change our point of view. We were having trouble with personal relationships, we couldn't control our emotional natures, we were a prey to misery and depression, we couldn't make a living, we had a feeling of uselessness, we were full of fear, we were unhappy, we couldn't seem to be of real help to people . . . When we saw others solve their problems by a simple reliance on the Spirit of the Universe, we had to stop doubting the power of God. Our ideas did not work. But the God idea did." (Big Book, p. 52)

On doubt and faith: "We agnostics and atheists were sticking to the idea that self-sufficiency would solve our problems.

When others showed us that 'God-sufficiency' worked
with them, we began to feel like those who had insisted the
Wrights would never fly.

"Logic is great stuff. We liked it. We still like it. It is not
by chance we were given the power to reason, to examine
the evidence of our senses, and to draw conclusions. That
is one of man's magnificent attributes . . . When we became
alcoholics, crushed by a self-imposed crisis we could not
postpone or evade, we had to fearlessly face the proposition
that either God is everything or else He is nothing. God
either is, or He isn't. What was our choice to be?

"Arrived at this point, we were squarely confronted with
the question of faith. We couldn't duck the issue. Some of
us had already walked far over the Bridge of Reason toward
the desired shore of faith. The outlines and the promise of a
New Land had brought lustre to tired eyes and fresh courage to flagging spirits. Friendly hands had stretched out in
welcome. We were grateful that Reason had brought us so
far. But somehow, we couldn't quite step ashore. Perhaps we
had been leaning too heavily on Reason that last mile and we
did not like to lose our support.

"That was natural, but let us think a little more closely.
Without knowing it, had we not been brought to where we
stood by a certain kind of faith? For did we not believe in our
own reasoning? Did we not have confidence in our ability to
think? What was that but a sort of faith? Yes, we had been
faithful, abjectly faithful to the God of Reason. So, in one

way or another, we discovered that faith had been involved all the time! . . . Had we not variously worshipped people, sentiment, things, money, and ourselves? And then, with a better motive, had we not worshipfully beheld the sunset, the sea, or a flower? Who of us had not loved something or somebody? How much did these feelings, these loves, these worships, have to do with pure reason? Little or nothing, we saw at last. Were not these things the tissue of which our lives were constructed? Did not these feelings, after all, determine the course of our existence? It was impossible to say we had no capacity for faith, or love, or worship. In one form or another we had been living by faith and little else." (Big Book, pp. 52–54)

On open-mindedness: "There is a principle which is a bar against all information, which is proof against all arguments and which cannot fail to keep a man in everlasting ignorance—that principle is contempt prior to investigation."

—Herbert Spencer (as quoted in the Big Book, p. 568)

Suggested Questions for Step Two

1. What does *beginning to believe in a Power greater than yourself* mean to you?
2. What does *sanity* mean to you?
3. Think of the areas of your life that you found to be unmanageable in Step One. How can sanity be restored to those areas?

4. What does it mean to you to have access to a
    Power greater than yourself?
5. When choosing a Higher Power, what qualities
    would you seek? Describe.

Step Three

Made a decision to turn our will and our lives over to the care of God as we understood Him.

Steps One, Two, and Three are also known as the ABCs of recovery. In this chapter we complete that first phase, and we also examine the Third Step requirements of decision, promise, and prayer.

In taking Step Three, we reaffirm our commitment to recovery, born out of Steps One and Two. As it says in the Big Book (page 58), "If you have decided you want what we have and are willing to go to any length to get it—then you are ready to take certain steps." Do you really want to take these Steps and submit yourself to this work? Are you willing to go to any lengths to have peace of mind? With this Step, we're completing the ABCs of Twelve Step recovery (adapted here for Double Trouble Step Three from page 60 of the Big Book). Let's look at these ABCs. We have seen

a. that we were alcoholics and/or addicts with a mental disorder and could not manage our own lives (Step One);

b. that probably no human power could relieve us of our dual diagnosis (Step Two);

c. that God could and would relieve us if He were sought (Step Three).

Now let's pause to apply these three ideas to ourselves and take responsibility for our own recovery. Let's restate them using "I" or our own name.

a. I couldn't manage my own life using drugs and alcohol; I was not taking care of my mental health.

b. No human power can relieve me of my suffering.

c. I am willing to believe that the God of my understanding can and will relieve me of my suffering if I seek Him.

If at this point you have any reservations about seeking help from the God of your understanding, please review the chapters covering the first two Steps. Spend as much time as you need there before going on.

Now we look at the requirements for taking Step Three. There is a common misconception here. *Deciding* to turn our will and our lives over to the care of God as we understand Him is not the same as *doing* it. The Third Step is a decision; we'll take action to carry out the decision in

Steps Four through Nine. All that is needed in Step Three is willingness, honesty, and faith. Ask yourself these questions: Why do I want to turn my will and my life over to the care of God as I understand Him? And how do I do that? Ask yourself, Why do I want to do this Step? Would anyone who thought his or her life was successful want to do this Step? If we thought our life ran successfully on our own will, we probably wouldn't turn it over. But the knowledge that we feel empty and unsatisfied with our lives, knowledge gained from taking Steps One and Two, prompts us to take this Step. Doesn't this make sense?

What does it mean to turn your will and your life over to God as you understand Him? What do you do? Before we came to DTR, our decisions were based on self-will. Was that the right way to run our lives? Running our lives on self-will is playing God, and it doesn't work. But how do we turn our will and lives over to the care of God? We begin with the Third Step decision, as stated in the Big Book (page 62): "We decided that hereafter in this drama of life, God was going to be our Director. He is the Principal; we are His agents. He is the Father, and we are His children." This is the keystone of the program that completes a triumphal arch through which we pass to freedom. To freedom. Are you seeking relief or are you seeking freedom? The Big Book continues (page 63), "We thought well before taking this step making sure we were ready; that we could at last utterly abandon ourselves to Him."

Most of us have balked at the idea of turning our will over to God. We turn it over, take it back, turn it over, take it back again. The Third Step shuffle dance is something we all do early on. But now, caring more about truth and freedom brings us to a decision. The commitment will come later in working Steps Four through Nine. Right now we make a decision, looking at the new roles we are going to play: We decide to be actors who seek not to run the show, but rather to be God's agents on the world's stage. God will be the director. We also decide to see ourselves as children of God; God will be the loving parent. Let us look at these roles. Can He be the director? Will you let Him be the loving parent? What does this mean to you? What will your role be? What will it mean to you to be a child of God? Each of us is a child of God. To be an agent of God, to be His child, and to know He is in charge is to live, not without fears, but free of the overwhelming power of fear. That is the promise of Step Three.

Still, the decision is hard to make. We need strength. We may find it in the Big Book's Third Step prayer (page 63):

God, I offer myself to Thee—to build with me and to do with me as Thou wilt. Relieve me of the bondage of self, that I may better do Thy will. Take away my difficulties, that victory over them may bear witness to those I would help of Thy Power, Thy Love and Thy Way of life. May I do Thy will always!

In this prayer, we are asked to give something up. But what are we really giving up? Something that didn't work anyway. And what do we gain? Something that is beautiful and worth having: a new beginning, a new life. Relinquishing self-will, the old self, is what Step Three offers us. Steps Four through Nine offer a prescription to free us from our old self-will. These Steps give us a way to transform our lives. What is so terrible about giving up our old lives anyway? They didn't work. When we turn our wills and our lives over to the care of our Higher Power, He fills the void. We are then reborn to something that's been inside us all along.

Some of us did believe there was a God, but we couldn't turn our will over to Him. We still thought we could do it ourselves. Some of us thought that God would punish us for our sins. Some of us found it unbearable to ask for God's guidance and help when we felt so worthless. We either believed we didn't need any help or we were afraid it would not come. At first, when we approached Step Three, the ideas of surrendering and "turning it over" were frightening. But by coming to meetings, listening to the experiences of others in DTR, practicing patience, and staying clean and sober, our consciences began to reawaken, and with this came hope. We began to accept our place in this world. We had no idea who God was or how to surrender to Him, but we found some relief in being clean and sober. In DTR we watched our fellows recover from severe mental disorders and emotional handicaps, heal broken hearts, and end estrangements from their families. After our experiences in jails and institutions, being homeless on the streets, eating out of garbage cans, being forced into treatment by the courts, we see that our Twelve Step program is simply the will of God being put into practical, everyday use. This spiritual experience is the realization that God will help us if we are completely honest in our efforts.

Sometimes our pride would not let us admit that we were ashamed of ourselves. Thus conflicted, we took our wills back and sent God out of our lives. How hard it was at times. We now understand that everything He sends our way is for our benefit. But it takes time to reach this understanding. Only in complete acceptance of the defeat of our pride and ego do we begin to grow. Each day we are challenged, sometimes with prosperity and sometimes with adversity. Too much prosperity can lead to complacency, and too much adversity breeds self-pity. Complacency and self-pity are two luxuries we cannot afford.

For years, before we came to believe, our resentments raged and we blamed God for all kinds of situations. If there was a God, why did He give us a mental disorder, with all the losses, adversity, and disappointments it brought us? But as we went to meetings and talked about our lives, we began to change our ideas of God, one day at a time. God had taken away from us our craving for drugs and alcohol and guided us into Twelve Step fellowship. We came into the fellowship with the understanding that we were different. We weren't like other people: we couldn't use drugs and alcohol as many people do, and we may need prescribed medications. From that moment, things began to change from within us.

Gradually, we came to recognize when we "got in our own way" because of our self-will. We could then choose to step aside and offer the situation to our Higher Power. We still resist letting His will into our lives. But where before there was no willingness, now there is some. For us, that is a great awakening, a great experience, to feel our suffering lessen from within. We now believe that we have played a large part in creating our own suffering. And that only by the grace of God will that ever change.

We pray to forgive ourselves, to learn to accept ourselves, to feel worthy and believe that we are human beings. Gradually, we let go of some of the old ways of looking at the world.

In the past, we couldn't do this. Living in fear kept us ignorant and stuck. Now we seek release from the inner turmoil that signals self-will. We seek release from our old overreactions to the everyday ups and downs of life. Now we have found a better way, and we ask for guidance and for the strength to follow it. If our thinking is okay, then our actions will be okay, and our lives will be okay. Trying to let God run our lives can be difficult. But we know that when we directed the show, we failed. Those of us who've let a Higher Power into our lives have seen our thinking, then our actions, and then our lives change dramatically for the better.

Making humble efforts to accept His will for us at difficult moments in life, we feel relieved of the burdens we
have carried. We ask Him for help. Our spiritual growth
cannot take place in us alone but only through the grace
that took us from the grips of active addiction and mental
disorders. Our old ways are still with us. We can still be very
self-destructive. But in admitting this, we feel released from
the bondage of self and gain entrance into the sunlight of
the spirit. There we can find the unconditional love that we
always have yearned for. There is the grace we need. This
is the miracle: our mental obsessions lift, and we discover a
new freedom of sanity, serenity, and sobriety.

A beginning is all that is needed. An opening. Anyone
can do it. The key is willingness. Self, or ego, will rear its
ugly head again and again, so we need to respond in the
moment with the willingness to "let go and let God." The
more we have faith in a Higher Power, the more indepen-
dent we find we can be. But we need to take certain actions,
to act on our faith. We need to make the decision. In times
of emotional disturbance or indecision, we can pause and in
stillness simply say the Serenity Prayer:

> *God, grant me the serenity to accept the things*
>   *I cannot change,*
> *courage to change the things I can,*
> *and wisdom to know the difference.*

We can add, "Thy will, not mine, be done." Soon we'll be ready for Step Four.

Relevant Quotes for Step Three

How it works: "Rarely have we seen a person fail who has thoroughly followed our path. Those who do not recover are people who cannot or will not completely give themselves to this simple program, usually men and women who are constitutionally incapable of being honest with themselves. There are such unfortunates. They are not at fault; they seem to have been born that way. They are naturally incapable of grasping and developing a manner of living which demands rigorous honesty. Their chances are less than average. There are those, too, who suffer from grave emotional and mental disorders, but many of them do recover if they have the capacity to be honest." (Big Book, p. 58) *Note:* The term "constitutionally incapable" *does not* refer to being diagnosed with a mental disorder. It refers to an inability to be honest with one's self, to tell oneself the truth about one's thoughts and experiences.

Step Three requirements: "The first requirement is that we be convinced that any life run on self-will can hardly be a success. On that basis we are almost always in collision with something or somebody, even though our motives are good. Most people try to live by self-propulsion. Each person is like an actor who wants to run the whole show; is forever trying to arrange the lights, the ballet, the scenery, and the rest of the players in his own way. If his arrangements would only stay put, if only people would only do as he wished, the show would be great." (Big Book, pp. 60–61)

The Step Three promises: "More and more we became interested in seeing what we could contribute to life. As we felt new power flow in, as we enjoyed peace of mind, as we discovered we could face life successfully, as we became conscious of His presence, we began to lose our fear of today, tomorrow or the hereafter. We were reborn." (Big Book, p. 63)

On taking action: "Next we launched out on a course of vigorous action, the first step of which is a personal house-cleaning, which many of us had never attempted. Though our decision was a vital and crucial step, it could have little permanent effect unless at once followed by a strenuous effort to face, and to be rid of, the things in ourselves which had been blocking us." (Big Book, pp. 63–64)

Suggested Questions for Step Three

1. What does it mean to you to decide to turn your will and your life over to the care of your Higher Power?

2. Which parts of your life are you willing to turn over to your Higher Power?

3. Which parts of your life are you unwilling to turn over to your Higher Power? What prevents you from giving them up?

4. What do you hope to experience as a result of your decision to turn your will and your life over to the care of your Higher Power?

Step Four

Made a searching and fearless moral inventory of ourselves.

Step Four is our Step to freedom. We take Step Four to identify our strengths and weaknesses, our character assets and liabilities. We do Step Four to get right with ourselves, and doing so is essential to our recovery. Ultimately, we seek to let go of the past and to learn tolerance, forgiveness, and acceptance of ourselves and of others.

In Step Four we'll review our lives in four areas: our mental symptoms, our resentments, our fears, and our sex issues. We'll make lists, or inventories, of our issues in each of those areas. In this Step we're searching fearlessly within ourselves with guidance from our Higher Power. Does that sound difficult? Remember, the rewards will be worth it. It may not seem this way at first, but Step Four, as challenging as it is, shows us a way of living that is easier than the way we lived before.

Still, the Step itself requires real, sustained effort. As we review our lives, we'll be sure it wasn't *our* desire to take a searching and fearless moral inventory of ourselves. It's true: this exercise is not easy. Some of it will likely be quite painful. If in writing down your moral inventory you reach a point where you can't go any further, put it down for the moment. As soon as you can, just pick up where you left off. Don't feel guilty for not doing the work all at once, but don't stop doing the work altogether either. Take your time, review the Suggested Directions at the end of this chapter, and have faith in a Power greater than yourself. Remember, none of us would be where we are in the program today if we acted solely on self-will. Please don't give up. Remember that this way lies freedom.

Before We Begin

Before beginning our inventories, let's warm up by making a list of the healthy things we do to feel good about ourselves. We'll refer to this list when we make our inventories. Then we can save it to use as a resource when we're feeling down.

Take a sheet of paper and make a list of healthy feel-good techniques. These are your coping strategies. Include in this list the nondestructive things that you do, or used to do, to get you through your darkest moments. How do you make yourself feel good or distract yourself from something or someone that sets you off? Do you call a friend? Listen to music, go for a walk, sit down and pray? When you're sad, do you distract yourself differently than when you're angry? Write all this down. If you have a hard time making this list, speak to other DTR members, or other people who know you, to share ideas about the various healthy ways you've learned to cope.

Our First Inventory: Mental Symptoms

Walking the road to self-awareness is scary when one has suffered from bipolar disorder, depression, schizophrenia, or other mental disorders. We naturally hesitate to examine what we've been trying to run away from all our lives. We want to avoid discomfort, and sometimes sitting in our mess seems most comfortable. So let's face our fears now. To prepare for the Fourth Step inventory, let's do an inventory of our mental symptoms. Remember, our mental disorders are not character flaws. We are not to blame for them. They are simply facts we need to deal with. Empowering ourselves in regard to our symptoms means finding ways to manage them ourselves, as many people do. (This does not mean dropping our medications, although many of us experience life-disrupting mood swings and hallucinations while on meds. Always take medicines as prescribed. If you have doubts or questions about them, discuss them with your doctor.)

You'll need several sheets of paper for this inventory. Divide each page into four columns by making vertical lines on the sheet.

Column 1: List Your Triggers

In the first column of this inventory, write your answers to these questions: What sets off your symptoms? What makes you anxious, angry, sad, or manic? Think about your environment: your home, the people around you, the neighborhood where you live. These things that set you off—people, situations, places, or things—are called "triggers." They get our mania going, or they get us anxious, angry, or sad. Make a list of your triggers.

Column 2: Describe Your Early Responses to Triggers

Now think about how you feel when you get triggered but are not yet out of control. Do you feel tight in the chest or have trouble breathing? Do you get a queasy stomach or racing thoughts? Think about your body and your mind. Don't just write "I feel anxious." How does anxiety feel to you? You might write: "I feel anxious: sweaty palms, fast heartbeat, poor concentration." Describe the bodily sensations and the thoughts that you experience when you get triggered but are not yet out of control. Write down these experiences and thoughts in column 2. You can also list your typical responses to other kinds of triggers not listed in column 1.

Column 3: Describe Your Out-of-Control Responses to Triggers

Now make a list of what happens if you don't deal immediately with those triggered feelings and you get out of control. That's what happens if you don't get off the merry-go-round of feelings. If you don't "nip it in the bud," things just get worse and worse until you become fully symptomatic and out of control. For example, you might become nervous in a social situation and, if left unchecked, your nervousness could turn into an anxiety attack.

Column 4: List Your Coping Strategies

For this column, look back at the list of healthy feel-good techniques you made earlier. Imagine how these techniques could help you nip a column-2 response in the bud, before it becomes a column-3 response. Now, in column 4, write down a healthy technique to use in each situation. For example, you might address your early anxiety symptoms by going for a run, calling a friend, or playing with your dog. Now, decide to use those strategies to distract yourself from a trigger before you let yourself get out of control.

Congratulations: you've done your first inventory, one that can help you cope with your mental symptoms and take charge of your life. It will begin to give you power over your symptoms without blaming yourself.

As with everything you read in this book, the symptom inventory just described is only a suggested set of directions. But it is tried and true: many have found it a valuable way to look at our symptoms and our coping strategies. For the whole truth about ourselves to be revealed, we have to write it down, to see it before us in black and white. It is important that we do this. Just thinking about it is not enough. When we put everything down on paper, we get a true picture of ourselves. We really have to face ourselves. And it takes courage to take a realistic, systematic look at ourselves, like a business taking inventory of its stock.

Our Higher Power will give us the guidance if we sincerely seek Him. We begin to know humility by removing the skeletons in our closet. We are released from anxiety and fear. We begin this work to gain self-respect, to stay alive, and to begin to know freedom from what troubles us. In doing our inventory, we develop the strength to help ourselves exchange self-pity and resentment for faith, hope, honesty, open-mindedness, and humility toward others and ourselves.

Our Fourth Step is an action-taking journey, and we can now feel a sense of confidence and protection from our Higher Power. Our first three Steps gave us hope and faith in a God of our understanding to guide us through a vigorous course of action that would launch us onto a healing path. With Step Four comes our first action: personal housecleaning. The Big Book (page 64) notes this transition: "Though our decision [in Step Three] was a vital and crucial step, it could have little permanent effect unless followed at once by a strenuous effort to face, and to be rid of, the things in ourselves which had been blocking us." Drugs and alcohol have been a smoke screen. Now, we want to get down to causes and conditions. We're about to continue with our inventories in the areas of resentments, fears, and sex issues.

We're journeying into ourselves to eliminate or minimize what hurts us and causes us our deepest problems, and to replace those things with something God-given and beautiful. This can be exciting and a great release. We find a life we might never have known.

But remember, we're not looking for perfection, only for a new start. As the Big Book says (on page 60), "We claim spiritual progress rather than spiritual perfection." We are always growing in understanding and effectiveness; this is a lifetime of work. Taking stock of ourselves honestly, we no longer have the need to fool ourselves. We come to see that most of our troubles are of our own making, most of our disappointments the result of our past refusal to know ourselves honestly. We see that we make ourselves victims. It is now our responsibility to be willing to move beyond this self-defeating behavior. In taking a personal inventory, we admit that we have problems (also known as character defects). Such disclosures, even to ourselves, can be painful and humiliating. This is not easy, and it takes commitment to begin. Before continuing to write your inventory, say a Third Step prayer to ask that your Higher Power's will be done: "Dear God, let me face the truth about myself, and help me get it down on paper. Help me see what I need to see about myself. When I stumble, do for me what I cannot do for myself."

Now you begin to take action; you begin to write your Fourth Step inventory (see the directions at the end of this chapter). It will come from within you, and as you pray, it will likely become easier. Go slow. Seek support. If you get triggered, seek the help you need. Doing your inventory, you gain a new perspective on yourself, and you begin to rid yourself of that which blocks you from experiencing joy and fulfillment in your life. Anger, fear, and pride try to beat you back every time. You may begin to tell yourself you don't need to do this work because you have been successful at stopping your drinking and drugging. But as you move forward with your inventory, you will see that in taking stock of yourself, you are gaining a new self-confidence and feeling a powerful sense of relief. You will begin to understand that while you do have character defects, they are defects you can work with. These are the rewards of Step Four.

We find another value in writing our inventories. There is good in us, and yet we may be afraid to know it or share it with anybody else. In our inventories, many of us write only about what's wrong with us. This might be our first attempt at writing about our qualities. For some of us it's really hard to see the good. And even if we see it, we aren't going to tell anybody about it. The core of our disease is a self-centeredness that distorts our perceptions of self and others.

But we need to think about our strengths in the same clear-eyed way we do about the things we want to change or improve. In doing so, we begin to develop a new sense of self-worth and integrity, and we begin to believe in ourselves. Allowing ourselves to feel our strengths is an important part of our recovery. Now we view ourselves honestly, both the good and the bad. This is no small matter. Just as we see a lot to admire in others in the program, we begin to develop those qualities and see them in ourselves too. And we realize they were always within us.

This marks the end of our Fourth Step inventory. We've looked at our terrible destructiveness, we've looked at our strengths, and we've gained new insights into ourselves and found ways to cope with our symptoms. We've learned tolerance, patience, and goodwill toward other people, even our enemies. In the words of the Big Book (page 71), "We hope you are convinced now that God can remove whatever self-will has blocked you off from Him. If you have already made a decision, and an inventory of your grosser handicaps, you have made a good beginning. That being so you have swallowed and digested some big chunks about yourself."

Relevant Quotes for Step Four

On resentment: "Resentment . . . destroys more alcoholics than anything else. From it stem all forms of spiritual disease, for we have been not only mentally and physically ill, we have been spiritually sick. When the spiritual malady is overcome, we straighten out mentally and physically. In dealing with resentments, we set them on paper. We listed people, institutions or principles with whom we were angry. We asked ourselves why we were angry. In most cases it was found that our self-esteem, our pocketbooks, our ambitions, our personal relationships (including sex) were hurt or threatened. So we were sore. We were 'burned up.'" (Big Book, pp. 64–65)

"It is plain that a life which includes deep resentment leads only to futility and unhappiness. To the precise extent that we permit these, do we squander the hours that might have been worth while." (Big Book, p. 66)

On fear: "This short word somehow touches about every aspect of our lives. It was an evil and corroding thread; the fabric of our existence was shot through with it. It set in motion trains of circumstances which brought us misfortune we felt we didn't deserve. But did not we, ourselves, set the ball rolling?" (Big Book, p. 67)

On faith and courage: "All men of faith have courage. They trust their God. We never apologize for God. Instead, we let Him demonstrate through us, what He can do. We ask Him to remove our fear and direct our attention to what He would have us be. At once, we commence to outgrow fear." (Big Book, p. 68)

On sex conduct: "We must be willing to make amends where we have done harm, provided that we do not bring about still more harm in so doing. In other words, we treat sex as we would any other problem. In meditation, we ask God what we should do about each specific matter. The right answer will come, if we want it . . . To sum up about sex: We earnestly pray for the right ideal, for guidance in each questionable situation, for sanity, and for the strength to do the right thing. If sex is very troublesome, we throw ourselves the harder into helping others. We think of their needs and work for them. This takes us out of ourselves. It quiets the imperious urge, when to yield would mean heartache." (Big Book, pp. 69–70)

Suggested Directions to Write a Step Four Inventory

Resentment Inventory

The Big Book calls resentment "the 'number one' offender" (page 64). Resentments destroy our spiritual connection, which is our one hope to recover. Resentments impede our healing process in recovery. When you write a resentment inventory, you will look at who and what you resent, what was done to you, how it affected you, and, most important, what your role was in each situation. You now take responsibility for your part in negative situations where previously you told yourself you were merely a victim.

Allow yourself plenty of paper for the Resentment Inventory: at least ten sheets, and possibly as many as forty. As you did for your symptoms inventory, draw vertical lines to divide each sheet into four columns. Save one or two blank sheets without columns for a separate list.

Before you sit down to write on these pages, we recommend that you say a prayer. It's a great tool to help you write from the gut, not the head. Center yourself and ask for guidance from your Higher Power before you proceed.

COLUMN 1: LIST THE PEOPLE, INSTITUTIONS, AND PRINCIPLES YOU RESENT

To begin, take the blank pages and simply list everyone and everything you're angry with or feel resentful about. The items for this resentment list should include people, institutions, and principles. It doesn't matter how long the list is; just empty out your gut, trusting whatever it is that may come out. Don't judge yourself by the number of resentments you have. Trust yourself and go with the flow of what comes. Thank God that what has been revealed on this list is your truth and your experience. Know that you can be free of it.

Making a list of people is relatively easy—people are people. But what about institutions? Think about the organizations you've encountered in your life: they might be hospitals, shelters, drug programs, bill collectors, Twelve Step programs, or other groups or organizations. And what are principles? Think of the values, sayings, or beliefs we were raised with or maybe still hear all the time, such as "what goes around comes around." Do you resent any of these? You might even resent some of the "rules to live by" from DTR or other fellowships. Put it all down on paper. You will know when you're finished.

Next, take one item from the list and write it in column 1 on one of your prepared pages. Do this for every resentment on your list, one resentment in column 1 of each sheet of paper. Get more paper if you need it.

Column 2: List Your Specific Resentments for Each

Next, you will add some details. In column 2 next to each name, list the things that person, institution, or principle did to harm you. Be honest, specific, and direct about the behaviors of others. Do this for each person, institution, or principle in column 1: list what each one did to you or failed to do for you, one at a time. For one person, you may have five resentments, five things you're angry at that person for. For a particular institution, you may have just one. Write what comes, listening to your gut, not your head. You may feel more anger as you review what these persons, institutions, and principles did and did not do. But continue until you have completed column 2 on each page for every person, institution, and principle on your initial list.

COLUMN 3: LIST THE EFFECTS ON YOUR SEVEN AREAS
OF SELF

Here you'll look at the effects of these situations on your
own life. What areas of your self were affected? The list
below shows the three basic human instincts, covering seven
areas of self. Choose which of those areas were affected by
each situation listed in column 2.

Basic Human Instincts and the
Seven Areas of Self

Social Instincts

1. Self-esteem: How we think or feel about
   ourselves
2. Pride: How we think or feel others define us
3. Personal relations: Relationships with other
   people
4. Ambitions: Our plans or goals for the future

Security Instincts

5. Emotional security: A general sense of well-
   being
6. Pocketbook: Money, property, and other
   necessities

Sex Instincts

7. Sex relations: Basic drive for sex, either selfish
   or intimate

Write in the third column all the areas of your self that were affected by the incident or situation. In some cases, almost all seven areas were involved in some way, but choose the most important ones. You will ask: Was my self-esteem affected by what person A did to me? Did it hurt or threaten my pride, my personal relations, or my ambitions? How about my emotional security, my pocketbook, my sex relations? Consider every area for each resentment.

COLUMN 4: LIST YOUR PART
Now go back to your list of people, institutions, and principles that you resent, the list that holds the key to your freedom. Can you look at the items on that list from a different angle? Look at column 3, the effects on you. Do you feel humiliated? Angry? Do you want revenge?

In the fourth column of this inventory, you are asked to turn away from such reactions. You are asked to look again at each party you resent (column 1), the specifics of each resentment (column 2), and each effect on you (column 3), and try to discern what your own part may have been in the situations in which you felt wronged. Were you selfish, inconsiderate, dishonest, frightened? To sort this out, you will need help from the God of your understanding, from a Power greater than yourself. It may be confusing at first, but stick with it. What was your role before, during, and after whatever caused the resentment? What actions and responsibilities did you forego? Did you take the easy way out? Did you blame others for matters that may not have been entirely their fault? Thank God, we are now aware that we are the makers of our own trouble. Ask yourself: In what ways was I responsible for what happened? Be as specific as you can. Ask: Where was I selfish? Where was I inconsiderate? Where was I frightened? Take your time, pray, stay focused, and keep writing. As you go, you'll begin to break through the lies you've told yourself in order to exist, to survive. These are lies that you no longer need to hold onto. Now that you have the support and love of the fellowship, it is no longer necessary to deceive yourself. We are all in this together.

After you've completed column 4, there will still remain plenty of incidents in which you truly were wronged, even if you had some part to play. How do you get free of these lingering feelings of anger and hurt? The Big Book has the answer (pages 66–67): "We realized that the people who wronged us were perhaps spiritually sick. Though we did not like their symptoms and the way these disturbed us, they, like ourselves, were sick too. We asked God to help us show them the same tolerance, pity, and patience that we would cheerfully grant a sick friend. When a person offended we said to ourselves, 'This is a sick man. How can I be helpful to him? God save me from being angry. Thy will be done.'"

In letting go of our anger and resentments, in turning them over to our Higher Power, we come to know a new freedom, a new awareness, a new truth. We begin to see how to free ourselves from what blocks us from the God of our understanding, from the sunlight of the spirit. We have a new tool to work on ourselves. We admit our wrongs honestly and are willing to set these matters right. What we thought was the truth turns into a lie, and that which we thought was a lie becomes the truth. And this is what will set us free. We thank God that we now understand we are the makers of our own problems; He doesn't make them for us. We are free from blaming other people, institutions, and principles.

Fear Inventory

Your fear inventory will show you how your life is shot through and through with fear. Fear can paralyze. Fear can stop us from moving ahead in our lives. Can fear be a conscious decision? As you write your fear inventory, you'll see that you've regularly made a conscious decision that in fact sets up every one of your fears. What is that decision? You choose to rely on yourself where fear is concerned, instead of relying on the God of your understanding. And from that decision, the fears only multiply.

This is not something any of us can swallow whole overnight; it is an idea that will take time to digest. None of us came to this conclusion all at once. But we did come to understand that we can no longer use false self-confidence to overcome fear. There has to be a better way. We need courage and faith, the opposites of fear, and we no longer have to apologize to anyone for seeking God's help. We are learning that spirituality is not a way of weakness but a way of strength. Faith will give us courage. We have come to believe, and now every time we experience fear, we ask God to remove our fear.

Again, we suggest beginning with a prayer. Humbly ask your Higher Power to guide you in the process of exploring your fears. Ask that He give you the strength and the insight to be searching and fearless in your quest. Know that He is on your side and will see you safely through the process if you only ask that He do so. Remember that it is nothing less than freedom from the past that you seek.

As you did for the Resentment Inventory, prepare some sheets of paper, each with three columns this time. Reserve a few blank pages, and use these to begin by making a list of all your fears. Write down whatever comes to mind. Fear of rejection, of pain, of being alone, of looking bad, of not getting what you want, of getting what you want, of feeling good, of feeling bad, of being with someone, of being alone; fear of having a mental disorder, of never recovering; fear of success, of failure, of not being good enough, of not having enough. We ask that you work on your list of fears until you know it's finished. If you need help getting started, look back at column 3 of your resentment inventory to see where you were frightened.

COLUMN 1: LIST YOUR FEARS

From your list, transfer each fear onto a separate sheet of three-column paper. Place it in column 1 and review all the sheets before continuing.

COLUMN 2: LIST WHAT'S BEHIND THOSE FEARS

Now you will seek out and write down what may be behind those fears. Look at each item in column 1, and write your thoughts about it in column 2. For example, you may fear going back into a hospital. You have written that fear in column 1 and now must ask yourself, "Why am I afraid of going back into a hospital? What is the source of that fear?" Think about it. Is humiliation involved? Potential harm? Are you afraid of what others would think? Are you afraid of how it would make you think about yourself? Would it bring up painful memories from the past? Would it make you feel hopeless? Again, take your time and write what you can about each fear. Let it spill out; try not to let your head censor whatever comes from the gut.

COLUMN 3: ADD FURTHER THOUGHTS ABOUT
THOSE FEARS

With the insight gained from what you wrote in column 2, think again about each fear listed in column 1. Ask yourself: Is the outcome you fear the result of a realistic wariness of potential damage or harm, or is it the remnant of some past experience that no longer has validity in the present? (Some people think of the word *fear* as an acronym for "false emotions appearing real.") Write your thoughts about this in column 3. You may want to list memories of incidents in the past from which the fear may have originated. Ask yourself: Is that the situation now, or has it changed? Am I afraid of something that is no longer the reality of the present?

Or you may write that you have no idea where the fear came from, that it seems to have always been with you. If so, ask yourself again: Just because I've always had this fear, does that mean it is real? Is it even my own fear, or did I pick it up from someone else, such as a parent?

Now we ask that you take these fears and turn them over to your Higher Power. Know that only He can take them away and that He will, if He is asked. The Big Book puts it this way (page 68): "We reviewed our fears thoroughly. We put them on paper . . . We asked ourselves why we had them. Wasn't it because self-reliance failed us? Self-reliance was good as far as it went, but it didn't go far enough. Some of us once had great self-confidence, but it didn't solve our fear problem, or any other. When it made us cocky, it was worse." The passage continues, "Perhaps there is a better way—we think so . . . We ask Him to remove our fear and direct our attention to what He would have us be. At once, we commence to outgrow fear."

Sex Relations Inventory

The next part of the inventory looks at sex, because we need to look at our conduct in that area too. "We all have sex problems," the Big Book points out (page 69). "We'd hardly be human if we didn't. What can we do about them?"

Our program does not tell us how to conduct our sex lives; rather it provides us with a set of spiritual tools to review and overhaul that part of our lives, as we did for resentments and fears. Each of us must decide what to do in that area. Let no one else tell you what to do. In this part of the inventory, you will review your relationships with other people and try to look honestly at the problems you caused for yourself and others. The Big Book provides guidance in taking an inventory of conduct in the area of sex, posing these questions on page 69: "Where had we been selfish, dishonest, or inconsiderate? Whom had we hurt? Did we unjustifiably arouse jealousy, suspicion or bitterness? Where were we at fault, what should we have done instead?" Now, armed with new knowledge, we are able to dispel old myths and beliefs about ourselves and our past behaviors and learn to act differently in our relationships.

For this inventory, you'll need a number of blank sheets of paper. No columns are needed. First make a list of your past and present sexual relationships and review the way you acted in each one. This is not about sex as much as it is about how you treat yourself and others in relationships. You will look at your part in relationship to those people. But first, pray for guidance and knowledge about your relationships. As the Big Book puts it (page 69), "We asked God to mold our ideals and help us live up to them."

Now take the first name on your list and write it on a separate sheet of paper. Then write a brief history of the relationship from beginning to end: how you got involved, what that person meant to you, the turning points in the relationship's development, how it ended, and, most importantly, the state of the relationship today. Then ask these nine questions, and answer in writing, honestly and fearlessly:

1. Where was I selfish?
2. Where was I dishonest?
3. Where was I inconsiderate?
4. Who was hurt? (Consider also the people indirectly related to the relationship such as friends, children, relatives, and so on.)
5. Where did I arouse jealousy?
6. Where did I arouse suspicion?
7. Where did I arouse bitterness?
8. Where was I at fault?
9. How should I have behaved instead?

As you answer these questions, take time to reflect on the nature of your relationship with the God of your understanding and what role that relationship did or did not have in each of your sexual relationships. Repeat the process for each of the relationships on your list.

Please find a quiet place in which to reflect on these questions, and take plenty of time to consider them fully. Always pray for guidance, for the understanding that what will be revealed will help you learn about healthier relationships and create the conditions in which you will be freed from the guilt and shame of the past.

Note: No suggested questions for Step Four are listed here, as they're included in the preceding Suggested Directions.

Step Five

Admitted to God, to ourselves, and to another human being the exact nature of our wrongs.

In the Fifth Step, we begin to accept ourselves. We more fully acknowledge our strengths and weaknesses, which we identified in our Step Four inventory. We recognize that our defects are still with us, and that we must name and understand them to set ourselves on a new path. We've begun to see our own self-deception and the trouble it's been causing us, but we don't yet know how to overcome it. Something more has to be done. That something is sharing. Using our Fourth Step inventory, we proceed to Step Five: we share about ourselves with another human being, holding back nothing, being willing to take suggestions and to accept directions. Because when we actually sit down and spill our guts aloud about our secrets, when we are honest with another person, then and only then can we know for certain that we have been honest with ourselves and with God.

Keeping the knowledge we gained in the Fourth Step to ourselves is not enough; it can even be dangerous. Wasn't it our "go-it-alone" thinking that got us into trouble in the first place? By talking to another person, especially someone with years in recovery, we benefit from that person's suggestions, insights, and experience. Although others' advice might be wrong in some details, in general it is more likely to help— in fact, it is crucial. We can't go it alone: we're just getting started with our program and with our contact with a Power greater than ourselves. How truly humbling an experience this can be! We suggest you pray for the courage it will require to take Step Five, for you will need the help of your Higher Power along with your own personal resolve in order to do it.

How do you choose the person with whom you take your Fifth Step? Take great care with this choice: that advice cannot be emphasized enough. When you share your Fifth Step, you are sharing your darkest secrets. Think what a hard time you had admitting them to God and even to yourself. You want to share your experiences with another human being who has done the same work, who has overcome serious difficulties and whose experience you can trust. If you have a DTR sponsor, that person might be a good choice, but you can consider others too. Should you pick someone who is dually diagnosed? It would be preferable, although is certainly not required. We strongly suggest that you find someone who understands what you're doing and why, preferably someone who has worked the program: if not DTR, then another Twelve Step program. Someone you can trust to keep in confidence what you say and, equally important, someone who can be objective and who will not be hurt by what you share about yourself and about your past. For that reason, we do not usually take our Fifth Step with our partners, spouses, close friends, or relatives. Pick someone who has already done this work, not someone who talks a good game. When you have selected the person with whom you want to take your Fifth Step, approach him or her and explain what you are trying to do and why. Most people will be willing to help.

From the book *Twelve Steps and Twelve Traditions*, we learn that *admitting* is a key word in Step Five. It asks of us to go counter to our alcoholic and addict tendencies. We saw the word *admitted* in Step One when we admitted powerlessness and first approached humility and honesty. In Step Five, the humility we gain by giving an honest accounting of ourselves before God and another human being is exactly what is needed to counter self-will. The self-deception we have long practiced needs to be overcome if we are to continue to recover.

This is easier said than done. We haven't generally let people know us. We have tried to live strictly on our own terms. We spent many years shutting people out, isolating and destroying relationships or being destroyed by them.

But we have to do the hard thing, as much as we may hate it. We have to share our inventory with someone else.

Some people in recovery never took their Fifth Step, and they manage to stay clean and sober and out of the hospital for long periods of time. But while they may be clean and sober, they are generally still filled with emptiness and misery, with resentments and despair. None of us likes to admit anything negative about ourselves. We have had a hard time trusting, and we now begin, slowly and with caution. First we share at meetings, and then we share our shortcomings with another person. Admitting the exact nature of our wrongs brings a change in us and sets us free.

We find that by sharing our Fourth Step inventory with God, ourselves, and another human being, we gain a better understanding of ourselves and perspective on our lives. We begin to build deeper, more trusting relationships. In the Fifth Step we let go of the loneliness and isolation. We no longer believe that we don't belong, that we're the only person in the world who feels the way we feel. Now that feeling can be replaced, maybe for the first time in our lives, with the knowledge that someone else truly understands us, who we are and what our struggles have been. As we allow another to listen to us and reflect on our strengths and weaknesses, we experience a new sense of mutuality, a sense of community.

We cannot have recovery and fellowship without admitting our powerlessness, without being willing to have a

Power greater than ourselves restore us to sanity. So after sharing our inventory with God and another human being, we review the Steps we've taken so far. Have we done the best we could? Have we been honest? Have we been thorough? We ask these questions to confirm our willingness to believe, our decision to turn our will and our lives over to the care of a God of our understanding, and most importantly, of the admission of powerlessness that we made in the First Step, which is the foundation of our recovery. "If we can answer to our satisfaction, we then look at Step Six," concludes the Big Book (page 76).

Recovery alone, without fellowship, is not enough; fellowship without recovery is not enough. We need both. When we share our recovery with our fellowship and listen to others' stories, we often discover common problems and common solutions. After taking our Fifth Step, we notice a new shift in our consciousness. We have gained a new freedom, a new sense of clarity. Before, we couldn't trust ourselves. Now we can trust and rely on our ability to be honest with ourselves and our Higher Power. We thank the God of our understanding for this shift in consciousness.

Relevant Quotes for Step Five

On taking the Fifth Step: "Having made our personal inventory, what shall we do about it? We have been trying to get a new attitude, a new relationship with our Creator, and to discover the obstacles in our path. We have admitted certain defects; we have ascertained in a rough way what the trouble is; we have put our finger on the weak items in our personal inventory. Now these are about to be cast out. This requires action on our part, which, when completed, will mean that we have admitted to God, to ourselves, and to another human being, the exact nature of our defects. This brings us to *the Fifth Step* in the program of recovery." (Big Book, p. 72)

On admitting to another person: "This is perhaps difficult—especially discussing our defects with another person. We think we have done well enough in admitting these things to ourselves. There is doubt about that. In actual practice, we usually find a solitary self-appraisal insufficient. Many of us thought it necessary to go much further. We will be more reconciled to discussing ourselves with another person when we see good reasons why we should do so. The best reason first: If we skip this vital step, we may not overcome drinking. Time after time, newcomers have tried to keep to themselves certain facts about their lives. Trying to avoid this humbling experience, they have turned to easier methods. Almost invariably they got drunk. Having persevered with the rest of the program, they wondered why they fell. We think the reason is that they never completed their housecleaning. They took inventory all right, but hung on to some of the worst items in stock. They only *thought* they had lost their egoism and fear; they only *thought* they had humbled themselves. But they had not learned enough of humility, fearlessness and honesty, in the sense we find it necessary, until they told someone else *all* their life story.

"More than most people, the alcoholic leads a double life. He is very much the actor. To the outer world, he presents his stage character. This is the one he likes his fellows to see. He wants to enjoy a certain reputation, but knows in his heart he doesn't deserve it.

"The inconsistency is made worse by the things he does on his sprees. Coming to his senses, he is revolted at certain episodes he vaguely remembers. These memories are a nightmare. He trembles to think someone might have observed him. As fast as he can, he pushes these memories far inside himself. He hopes they will never see the light of day. He is under constant fear and tension—that makes for more drinking." (Big Book, pp. 72–73)

On selecting someone for our Fifth Step: "We must be entirely honest with somebody if we expect to live long or happily in this world. Rightly and naturally, we think well before we choose the person or persons with whom to take this intimate and confidential step. Those of us belonging to a religious denomination which requires confession must, and of course, will want to go to the properly appointed authority whose duty it is to receive it. Though we have no religious connection, we may still do well to talk with someone ordained by an established religion. We often find such a person quick to see and understand our problem. Of course, we sometimes encounter people who do not understand alcoholics.

"If we cannot or would rather not do this, we search our acquaintance[s] for a close-mouthed, understanding friend. Perhaps our doctor or psychologist will be the person. It may be one of our own family, but we cannot disclose anything to our wives or our parents which will hurt them and make them unhappy. We have no right to save our own skin at another person's expense. Such parts of our story we tell to someone who will understand, yet be unaffected. The rule is we must be hard on ourselves, but always considerate of others.

"Notwithstanding the great necessity for discussing ourselves with someone, it may be one is so situated that there is no suitable person available. If that is so, this step may be postponed, *only, however, if we hold ourselves in complete readiness to go through with it at the first opportunity* [italics added]. We say this because we are very anxious that we talk to the right person. It is important that he be able to keep a confidence; that he fully understand and approve what we are driving at; that he will not try to change our plan. But we must not use this as a mere excuse to postpone.

"When we decide who is to hear our story, we waste no time. We have a written inventory and we are prepared for a long talk. We explain to our partner what we are about to do and why we have to do it. He should realize that we are engaged upon a life-and-death errand. Most people approached in this way will be glad to help; they will be honored by our confidence.

"We pocket our pride and go to it, illuminating every twist of character, every dark cranny of the past." (Big Book, pp. 73–75)

The Fifth Step promises: "Once we have taken this Step, withholding nothing, we are delighted. We can look the world in the eye. We can be alone at perfect peace and ease. Our fears fall from us. We begin to feel the nearness of our Creator. We have had certain spiritual beliefs, but now we begin to have a spiritual experience. The feeling that the drink problem has disappeared will often come strongly. We feel we are on a Broad Highway, walking hand in hand with the Spirit of the Universe." (Big Book, p. 75)

After the Fifth Step—surveying our work: "Returning home we find a place where we can be quiet for an hour, carefully reviewing what we have done. We thank God from the bottom of our heart that we know Him better. Taking this book down from our shelf we turn to the page which contains the twelve steps. Carefully reading the first five proposals we ask if we have omitted anything, for we are building an arch through which we shall walk a free man at last. Is our work solid so far? Are the stones properly in place? Have we skimped on the cement put into the foundation? Have we tried to make mortar without sand?" (Big Book, p. 75)

Suggested Questions for Step Five

1. What prevents you from admitting your short-comings to another person?

2. Why do you resist sharing your life story, including your mental disorder, with another person?

3. How will you go about admitting your short-comings to your Higher Power?

4. To whom is it most difficult to acknowledge your shortcomings: to yourself? to another person? to your Higher Power?

5. If you admit the truth about your mental disorder to God, to yourself, and to another person, how might it help you accept and understand yourself?

6. What do you hope to experience as a result of admitting to yourself, to another person, and to God the truth about yourself?

Step Six

Were entirely ready to have God remove all these defects of character.

Having been granted a release from drugging and drinking, and beginning to adapt our lives to maintaining our mental health, we hope to achieve, by the same means, a release from other difficulties or defects. And why not? We have enough willingness and honesty. Indeed, with those qualities we have come a long way on our journey, spiritually and in building character.

Step Six shows us more humility. We saw in ourselves dishonesty and selfishness. We saw ourselves frightened, inconsiderate, and self-centered. Now we see how those parts of our character created our problems. With those habits of mind we created problems for other people as well, and they sometimes then hurt us, causing us to have more fear, resentment, remorse, and guilt. These parts of ourselves are still potentially with us, but now we see their true cost. With Step Six we ask if we are ready to let go of them.

Admitting anything unpleasant about one's self is an ego-deflating, humbling experience for anyone—all the more so for addicts and alcoholics with mental disorders who often maintain a particular combination of egoism and self-loathing. But the humility we gained through discovering ourselves and bringing our truths to the God of our understanding and to another human being—that was exactly what we needed to counter the self-centeredness, self-justifications, and rationalizations we have lived with for so long.

We can turn to page 68 of the book *Twelve Steps and Twelve Traditions* (also known as the "Twelve and Twelve") to read more about the challenge of Step Six. Do we aim for "only as much perfection as will get us by in life," or do we aim even higher? That difference, the passage continues, is "the difference between striving for a self-determined objective and for the perfect objective which is of God." If that challenge sounds daunting, remember that the only requirement is to make a beginning and keep trying.

Are we ready? We might not be ready to let go of our old behaviors or beliefs, even if we recognize what they're doing to us. In that case, we ask God to help us be willing in Step Six. We begin Step Six by recognizing that self cannot overcome self. We have lived with our self-serving, self-centered behavior almost our whole lives. We have become comfortable with the pain and have learned to handle it in a fashion. Taking a chance on changing can be unsettling: we don't know what the future will bring and what we might face. Thus, this Step is very difficult for some of us. With Step Six, we are growing from a person who has doubt to a person with faith. Growing from a dishonest person to an honest one, from a selfish person to an unselfish person. Growing from a self-serving person to one who is interested in others. We may wonder, how are we going to get what we want? Who is going to take care of us? If God, in His grace, removes our character defects, will we still have a personality? If God takes away those qualities we have found objectionable about ourselves, will things be much better than before?

We can tell you this: the God of your understanding will replace them with so many better things for you, you'll wonder what took you so long. But you'll never know that transformation unless you first are willing. Willingness is the key to working this Step. If you are not ready, pray for the willingness to become entirely ready to have God remove your defects of character. Do you know that you cannot save yourself? Do you realize that He can and He will? If you've seen how your best intentions can go wrong, can you come to believe in God's will for you instead? If you don't, your mind closes to the possibility of God's grace for you. So stop for a moment and review your past, the proof that a life run on self-will cannot be a success. Pray for help in becoming ready to relinquish that kind of life. It is then you will be shown the possibility of your God's will for you.

Having done the work of Steps One through Five, we now continue to venture ahead on our recovery journey. Humility means facing our shortcomings honestly, but it doesn't mean thinking less of ourselves than we ought to. We acknowledge that we do certain things well, and we respect and accept ourselves for that. We come to learn that we can't always be the center of the universe. When we were drinking, drugging, and spiritually unhealthy, we were consumed by pride and self-centeredness. Humility teaches us self-acceptance and self-respect in the face of our character defects. It can help us to have a healthy dependence on the God of our understanding, Who will help us overcome our obstacles and imperfections so that we may grow and progress spiritually.

Situations will arise that will destroy our serenity—for the moment. The pain we feel might lead us to seek God for help. Accepting our part in every situation, we can pray to understand how our character defects contributed to it. We can ask ourselves: Were we patient? Were we looking for our own way? Answers to these questions can lead us to learn to put our self-reliance aside and to humbly ask God to remove our shortcomings. Situations may not change, life circumstances might not change, but as we practice understanding and work toward self-acceptance, we gain peace and serenity: the benefits of placing our reliance on a Power greater than ourselves.

At this point, we should ask ourselves honestly about this relationship with the God of our understanding that we claim is so important. How painful has it been to stop trying to control our own and others' lives? How comfortable is it now to accept life on its own terms, to accept the difficulties and challenges we face? We are giving Him our fear, our anger, our anxiety, our uncertainty and worry, and we are being healed by knowledge, by the spiritual strength we have received, by the mental and emotional security we find in a Power greater than ourselves. We remind ourselves that we strive for spiritual progress, not perfection.

In Step Six, we look at our inventories: what do we see there that we are still unwilling to let go? It may be uncomfortable to admit that after everything we've been through, we still feel attached to some of our character defects. So we learn to sit with this knowledge until we are willing to let go. We'll never move past where we are until we honestly admit where we are. We ask ourselves these questions: Can self-will eliminate self-will? Can we will or wish away those objectionable parts of ourselves that might cause us shame, guilt, and remorse, those parts that might trigger us to use drugs and alcohol or be anxious, manic, depressed, and so on? Have we found the faith and hope to become ready to have the God of our understanding help us? Do we believe He will do for us what we could not do for ourselves? Will He help us as we are, people with a mental disorder and a substance abuse problem? Can He take away our pain and ease our struggles? We ask God to remove these parts of self that we cling to. We learn that when we become entirely ready, at that point we can move on. It is not later, after we are fixed and better and changed people, that we are ready to come to the God of our understanding. It is now, at Step Six in our path toward recovery.

Relevant Quote for Step Six

On readiness: "We have emphasized willingness as being indispensable. Are we now ready to let God remove from us all these things which we have admitted are objectionable? Can He now take them all—every one? If we still cling to something we will not let go, we ask God to help us be willing." (Big Book, p. 76)

Suggested Questions for Step Six

1. Review your list of your shortcomings. Which shortcomings are you not ready to have removed? How do they help you? How do they hurt you?

2. What is interfering with your readiness (willingness) to have God remove your shortcomings?

3. What is the best possible attitude that you can have to make a beginning of this lifelong job of letting go of the fear to have your shortcomings removed? Describe.

4. What needs to happen for you to be ready to ask God to remove your shortcomings?

Step Seven

Humbly asked Him to remove our shortcomings.

In Step Six, we became willing to let go of these character defects and the associated behaviors that we have found objectionable; we became willing to take the chance in spite of ourselves and to struggle with our own ambivalence about it. Now, when we are entirely ready, we might say a prayer, as suggested in the Big Book (page 76): "My Creator, I am now willing that you should have all of me, good and bad. I pray that you now remove from me every single defect of character that stands in the way of my usefulness to You and my fellows. Grant me the strength, as I go out from here, to do your bidding. Amen." The passage continues, "We have now completed Step Seven."

The spiritual foundation of Step Seven is humility. Our shortcomings can be placed in God's care and be removed. All of ourselves, good and bad, we give to God. We don't decide which defects get removed. Wouldn't that be easy? We don't decide the order in which they are removed. We ask God to decide which defects stand in the way of our usefulness to Him and to others. And then and only then, by giving all of ourselves, do we let Him remove the bad and return the good to us.

But as we learn in the Christian Bible (James 2:20), "faith without works is dead." We are now ready to move on to Step Eight; more action is necessary for us to improve on our journey of recovery from dual-diagnosis.

Relevant Quote for Step Seven

"We began to get over the idea that the Higher Power was a sort of bush-league pinch hitter, to be called upon only in emergency. The notion that we would still live our own lives, God helping a little now and then, began to evaporate." (Twelve and Twelve, p. 75)

Suggested Questions for Step Seven

1. What does *humility* mean to you?
2. What do you hope to experience as a result of asking God to remove your shortcomings?
3. What would your life be like if you didn't ask God to remove your shortcomings?

Step Eight

Made a list of all persons we had harmed, and became willing to make amends to them all.

Looking back over our inventories, we survey the wreckage of our past and make the effort to consider the people we have hurt and how we hurt them. It's not easy to examine our broken relationships and the obstacles blocking us from forgiveness, both toward ourselves and others. At first, we might become defensive. We might focus only on what others have done, and in some situations rightly so. But we are called to realize that we have hurt others with our drinking or drugging, our mania, depression, anxiety, or hallucinations. We may have hurt them inadvertently in our mental illness, which is beyond our control. But we must recognize that we have damaged or destroyed our relationships with those around us. We have harmed people, intentionally or unintentionally, and ought to make amends. So Step Eight calls us to make the list of people we have harmed, starting with those who have most meaning to us. In Step Nine, we will seek the strength to do something about it, so we might enjoy a more peaceful recovery. But first, we must diligently search our memories for all the people we have harmed, and simply write their names on a sheet of paper.

By facing up to the truths of our past, as we did in Step Four, we can give real meaning to our experiences, whether we consider them good or bad ones. However painful some of them may be, as we reflect on our past, we come to really know ourselves intimately, perhaps for the first time. In Step Eight, however, we focus not on our shortcomings but on the people who were affected by those shortcomings. And we don't forget to include ourselves on our list, as we clearly have done great harm to ourselves.

For the time being, we set aside any thoughts of making amends, and even the question of our willingness to make amends. When we're ready for that, we'll know it, and we'll have the power to face the catastrophes of our past. But for now, easy does it. For now we make progress by simply writing our list. We are careful to include each person's name and exactly what we did to cause that person harm.

Then we move from our head to our heart, easing the internal argument between fear and pride that often comes up in doing this work. We quiet the whirlwinds of resentment and fear. We focus on a new faith that our Higher Power, working through the Steps and the Fellowship, will carry us from spiritual bankruptcy to a life of freedom from the guilt and shame of our past, just as He is doing with our character defects. Making the list is another Step toward freedom. If we feel unwilling to do so, we ask our Higher Power for help. We pray for willingness and strength to face the past until, one day, we find that it has arrived. But we must do our part; our Higher Power does not work through us unless we humbly ask. So we ask, every day, every hour if need be. Remember, at the beginning, we made a commitment to go to any length for our recovery. Every Step we take in our recovery brings us back to the understanding that we don't want to move backwards, we don't want to drink and drug and suffer pain and lose our emotional serenity. So with the support of our Higher Power and the guidance of those in the DTR fellowship, we pray for the power to make the list of all the persons we have harmed. And then we do it.

The second part of Step Eight is about gaining the willingness to make amends to everyone on the list. We don't have to actually make the amends at this time; we don't even have to think about how to go about it. We have made the list, and that in itself represents great spiritual progress. We are actively taking responsibility for all our behaviors. We may not have realized how other people were affected by our behaviors, but we have come to realize it now. Now, we must become willing to make amends. We understand that we must do this for the sake of our own recovery.

When we ask to become willing to make amends, we need to be thoroughly open. With the help of our Higher Power, we need to take the risks necessary to move toward our spiritual goal of ridding ourselves of self-will. Being sorry is not enough. "To make amends" means to "make whole." It is not enough just to apologize; we must become willing to change our thinking, attitude, and behavior toward those we have harmed. These changes will be necessary if we are to make whole again the damage we have caused. So our willingness to make amends includes being willing to make emotional and behavioral changes in ourselves. In doing so, we begin to understand the impact of our behaviors on others.

Can you do it? If you are uncertain, ask yourself once again: How free do I want to be? If you want to be free of the pain, guilt, and shame, you will decide to ask your Higher Power for the willingness to help you move along in the spiritual journey so that one day you can live as a free person in the present rather than as a slave to the past.

With Step Eight, we are brought to a place inside ourselves where we can see how insensitive we have been and how hard it is to relate to other people, to have empathy, understanding, and love. We begin to forgive ourselves and others. We start to believe that perhaps we can be loved and forgiven in return. We realize it might be possible for us to learn how to be there for other people, to take part in their lives, to experience less guilt, shame, and remorse. We become free to heal ourselves by offering healing to others. Our past can destroy our present and keep us chained to our disease and its consequences. Could our amends free us from the past so we can live today? Could making amends set us free to stay clean and more in control of our symptoms?

Making amends will lead to emotional freedom. It will end our isolation from our fellows and from God. We are putting our lives in order and becoming spiritually fit to be of service to our Higher Power and to the people in our lives. In writing our Step Eight list and becoming willing to make amends, we ask our Higher Power to guide us to do the best we can with this task, as long as there still are people hurt by what we have done. We pray for guidance. If we are right with the God of our understanding and with ourselves, then we will know the experience of getting right with the world and the people in it.

Again, how free do we want to be? It is painful to pause and to look back on the wreckage of our past and to discover where we have been at fault, realizing that those in our past whom we have harmed stand between us and our desire to move forward. There really seems no other way to do it. None of us really wants to make restitution, but can we have peace and serenity if we don't? We don't think so. We have to ask for courage to face those persons who still live in our conscience, to deal with the damage we've done by being willing to make amends to them all. We now go on to Step Nine.

Suggested Directions for Step Eight

To start our Step Eight list, we review our lists from Step Four. When we inventoried our resentments, fears, and sexual relationships, we wrote down the names of many people who perhaps belong on our new list, our list of those we have harmed. These are people we resent, people we have hurt in relationships, people we have harmed by action, inaction, or retaliation. Other names will come to us now, too, names that had not appeared in our Fourth Step. Just as with our inventories, we'll know when the list is completed.

Now we go through the list person by person. To whom are we willing to make amends? To whom are we unwilling to make amends—at least, not yet? Willingness can take time. Don't try to change what comes to mind, just write yes or no, willing or unwilling, next to each name.

How will we gain the willingness to do it? By making the amends we are willing to make initially, our willingness to make the next one will grow. As we write down each name, we ask ourselves: Am I willing to do whatever this person might ask to right the wrong (as long as it does not hurt myself or others)? We also ask: Aside from the willingness question, how will I get in touch with or find this person? Then we write down the harm we have done to that person. And that goes further than simply writing "I was self-centered." We get down to specifics; for example: I lied to you about this; I gossiped about you; I stole from you; I did this; I failed to do that. Put down on paper everything you are aware of that you did to each person.

Relevant Quote for Step Eight

"First, we take a look backward and try to discover where we have been at fault; next we make a vigorous attempt to repair the damage we have done; and third, having thus cleaned away the debris of the past, we consider how, with our newfound knowledge of ourselves, we may develop the best possible relations with every human being we know.

"This is a very large order. It is a task which we may perform with increasing skill, but never really finish . . . This reopening of emotional wounds, some old, some perhaps forgotten, and some still painfully festering, will at first look like a purposeless and pointless piece of surgery. But if a willing start is made, then the great advantages of doing this will so quickly reveal themselves that the pain will be lessened as one obstacle after another melts away." (Twelve and Twelve, pp. 77–78)

Suggested Questions for Step Eight

1. What is making it difficult for you to put certain people on your list? Explain.

2. How does your resistance to forgiving yourself or others block you in your relationship with yourself, your Higher Power, and with other people?

3. How will making amends set you free and help you to grow spiritually?

Step Nine

Made direct amends to such people wherever possible, except when to do so would injure them or others.

We have become willing to make our amends to the people we have harmed, willing to go to any lengths for our recovery and to build our new lives. Moving on to Step Nine, we continue to grow on our spiritual path. Without the guidance and strength of a Higher Power, it would be impossible to proceed through these stages of reconstructing our lives. The God of our understanding works for us and through us. He did for us what we could not do for ourselves, removing the compulsion to drink and drug and helping us to take care of our mental health. We continue to seek His guidance.

Taking action in Step Nine can and will affect other people. We cannot do anything about it until we have shared it with God, ourselves, and our sponsor. This is not about us feeling good at the expense of destroying someone else's life. We realize that we might have to live with our guilt and remorse for a while if acting in haste has the potential to hurt someone else, causing more harm than good.

Step Nine suggests what to do and when. We make *direct* amends. We make them *wherever* possible. It also tells us to refrain from doing so when it would injure someone. "We subjected ourselves to a drastic self appraisal," as the Big Book puts it (page 76). "Now we go out to our fellows and repair the damage done in the past."

We are reminded once again that we are willing to go to any length for our recovery. This brings us back to the reason why we're doing our work: so we can live a life clean and sober and mentally healthy. We are still consciously aware of our potential problems with drinking and drugging and mental disorders. We seek to reach a place where we can confidently say that we live in the present, no longer haunted by our past. This is the reason for Step Nine. Making our amends, we are consciously aware of repairing the injuries we have caused others. It was hard for us to look at how we have hurt others, how self-centered we were, thinking only of how we could feel better. But now we are involving other people and our Higher Power. Running our lives on self-will hurt others and isolated us from God and humanity. Making amends frees us to find compassion, to connect with others, and to live a better life.

We will know when we are ready to make amends. We have been preparing ourselves to do so by seeing the harm we did and planning what to say to the people we have hurt.

We've discussed our plans with our sponsor, and we follow our sponsor's suggestions to protect others from still further harm. We look over our list from Step Eight and pray for the willingness to move forward, to be unafraid. To have that courage, we ask for help from our Higher Power to make restitution, the spiritual foundation of Step Nine.

Our amends may not always be accepted, but after we are done, we can walk away a freer person. If we leave the outcome in the hands of the God of our understanding, our task in Step Nine is about doing the work of cleaning up the wreckage of our past so that we will not go backward and possibly relapse to drinking or drugging. Whatever the situation is that calls for amends, we have to do something about it. If it is about money, asking forgiveness of an enemy, facing a domestic problem or a crime, something will have to be done. We want to go on with our lives and be able to look people in the eye. By cleaning up our past, we can live in the present. We can look in the mirror, forgive ourselves, and ask other people to forgive us. We can come face-to-face with ourselves. We are no longer afraid that our past will catch up with us. We become more useful to God, to ourselves, and to our fellows. As long as our past is unresolved, we cannot live in the present. Never again having to betray ourselves and no longer betrayed by our thoughts, emotions, and actions, we can trust and be trusted. We have found freedom. A spiritual path is not a theory: we must live it!

Suggested Directions for Step Nine

Whenever possible, amends should be made in person, face to face. Only if it is absolutely impossible to meet in person do we consider making amends on the telephone. A letter is a last resort, although it is appropriate for making amends to people who have died or cannot be located.

In planning our amends, we consider what we will tell each person about why we are here. We tell him or her what has changed in our lives that brought us to this point—as much as we want to share. We recall with the person the harm we believe we have done, and we sincerely apologize. We then ask each person if there is anything they need to say to us, and then we just sit and listen, without back talk or contradiction. Having heard them out, we ask if there is anything we can do to right this wrong. And we ask the person if he or she can forgive us.

The Big Book gives us specific suggestions for making various types of amends to our families, to friends, for money and business matters, for criminal offenses. We start with the amends we are willing to make and the people we can find. We pray beforehand for the strength and wisdom to do what we need to do to the best of our ability. Remember, we are not to be reckless and risk hurting others. We pray for the readiness to take responsibility for our past and responsibility for the well-being of others at the same time. We ask for help in being considerate of other people's feelings and using good sense, especially in practical matters of restitution.

We are careful not to skip over what we find hard or humiliating to do. This is no time for excuses. It is a real opportunity: we have a chance to right a wrong. The rule is to disclose all harm. There will be some people on our list we need to leave alone; sometimes that will be the best amends we can make. When we look at our list with our sponsor, we may find names that no longer need to be there. We make amends to ourselves by stopping drinking, drugging, and abusing ourselves. We begin to live our new lives in recovery, working and living a spiritual program to the best of our ability. We see that to forgive ourselves is important as we go about asking others to forgive us.

When making amends to our family members, we need to use discretion: being too direct may hurt them even more than we already have. We need to be considerate in bringing up situations that would cause unnecessary pain, and wary of telling them about experiences we've had that they know nothing about. We do not hurt or sadden our family members by unloading to them about our past drugging and drinking and hospitalizations. We share these experiences *only* with someone who could understand. We are hard on ourselves but considerate of others. We are careful not to inflict additional harm on others to relieve our own guilt. Our sponsors will guide us in making amends to our family members and the people closest to us.

Our actions speak louder than any words ever can, and so we are also to right our wrongs by the way we conduct ourselves in our new lives. We do whatever is necessary to release us from our past and do no more harm. We open new doors for ourselves, remembering that old behaviors and habits die hard. We go to others in a forgiving and considerate spirit. We admit our faults. We do not criticize or blame. We are to discuss our own faults, not the faults of others, and reach within for strength to clear the wreckage of our past.

Financial amends can be hard for us. We may have debts, missed child support payments, overdue rent, and overdrawn credit. We really don't want to make financial amends, but we do. Our drugging and drinking has made us slow to pay. We make the best deal we can. Some of us have to budget our money very carefully to start making financial restitution. We speak with our sponsor and those to whom we owe money to work out a payment plan. We must lose our fear, because fear might take us back to drinking and drugging. Once we have made amends to those people we had harmed, we try not to repeat the past. We stop messing with other people. We learn to be helpful and to mind our own business.

Some of us will have to deal with past criminal offenses. As with all other amends, we do not shrink from our responsibility. With criminal offenses, we must be very clear as to what we must do. After writing our amends about a criminal act, we ask for strength and direction to do the right thing. We make sure to sit down with someone to get clear about not doing more harm. But we must not stop there. We go to any lengths for our recovery, no matter what. We may even need to face jail time, losing our job and reputation, but we must be willing. We consult with lawyers, our sponsors, and anyone else whose knowledge might help us in this situation. The Big Book puts it this way (page 80): "If we have obtained permission, have consulted with others, asked God to help and the drastic step is indicated, we must not shrink." But again, remember, we take no action if doing so might hurt other people.

Relevant Quote for Step Nine

"After we have made the list of the people we have harmed, have reflected carefully upon each instance, and have tried to possess ourselves of the right attitude in which to proceed, we will see that the making of direct amends divides those we should approach into several classes. There will be those who ought to be dealt with just as soon as we become reasonably confident that we can maintain our sobriety. There will be those to whom we can make only partial restitution, lest complete disclosure do them or others more harm than good. There will be other cases where action ought to be deferred, and still others in which by the very nature of the situation we will never be able to make direct personal contact at all." (Twelve and Twelve, p. 83)

Suggested Questions for Step Nine

1. What is your resistance to making amends?
2. Which amends on your list are causing you the most difficulty? Explain.
3. How will you forgive yourself? What is your resistance to forgiving yourself?
4. What are your feelings and experiences after making your first amend? Describe.

Step Ten

Continued to take personal inventory and when we were wrong promptly admitted it.

Through our Steps so far, we have been relieved of many of our life problems. We now look to maintain our recovery: we want to continue this way of living, and so we strive for it on a daily basis. For the dually diagnosed, staying in recovery requires maintaining new habits. Step Ten guides us to stay in the spirit of our new ways of admitting and handling our mistakes. Any new mistakes we make, we promptly set right.

The Tenth Step is also a Step of spiritual growth. We have had a spiritual awakening and now we proceed to develop. We become more effective and more understanding. Willing to grow, we continue to look at our selfishness, dishonesty, resentments, and fears. When these come up, we ask the God of our understanding to remove them. We learn love and tolerance for our fellows, working our Steps to the best of our abilities. We can better recognize our feelings in the present and see what's behind them. When another person is involved, we ask ourselves, what might we have done to this person? What aspect of our self was affected—self-esteem, personal relationships, material or emotional well-being, ambitions, sex instinct, pride? What shortcoming of ours was involved? We have come to learn, when we resent or are afraid, not to act on these feelings immediately, but to ask our Higher Power for guidance. We have learned to recognize when we've hurt another human being and to make amends promptly. We know that when we are disturbed, we need to look at ourselves. Even when another person might have wronged us, we can only deal with our own feelings and actions. We step back and look at what upset us. We look for the cause, correct our own mistakes, and work on our attitudes. This is a tough job, but as long as we make the effort, look to understand our part, and make a self-appraisal, we will progress, knowing that this is a good job well done.

Taking a daily personal inventory makes our lives easier. We take some time out of our busy day and look at how we have conducted ourselves, doing a mental inventory, and, if we wish, writing down our observations. We continue to watch for dishonesty, for selfishness, for resentment and fear. We may have had trouble admitting when we were wrong. The reward of this Step is that by catching problems early, we avoid all that built-up garbage. Addressing our mistakes gets easier as we become aware of the price we pay when we don't admit we are wrong. We come to value living in the present. By making amends immediately for harm we have done, we avoid having to do it later and feeling guilty in the meantime. We turn to helping others, not hurting them. Love and tolerance are our code, and we become comfortable with ourselves. We stop making ourselves suffer unnecessarily and stop punishing ourselves and others. We will make mistakes our whole lives, but the more we practice this Step, the more freedom we gain.

When we practice Step Ten on a daily basis, self-searching becomes a habit. We want to take responsibility for our actions. Taking daily inventory enables us to let go of the past and to make peace with ourselves and others. Step Ten is about facing our self-obsession, not promoting it. We don't write our daily inventory when we feel like beating ourselves up, but only after we have regained our balance. No doubt we need to rid ourselves of our self-centered, self-serving motives. But we have had a daily reprieve from drug or alcohol use and were given the opportunity to work on our mental health. With these gifts, we can be of service to the God of our understanding in all our activities. "Thy will, not mine, be done."

What about the harm done to us? Aren't we entitled to be angry? It's hard not to be, especially when we are not at fault. But we look inside ourselves and ask for the willingness to forgive. We seek to let go. It's often difficult, but don't be discouraged. We are good people, trying our best to live along spiritual lines. Believe that. We look for strength and guidance from the God of our understanding to see us through. In the words of the Serenity Prayer, "God, grant me the serenity to accept the things I cannot change, courage to change the things I can, and wisdom to know the difference." We pray for self-acceptance. We strive not for perfection, but for progress. We need to get right and stay right with the God of our understanding and with ourselves and others. We discipline ourselves to step back and to think, even in difficult or uncomfortable situations. Pain is the touchstone of spiritual progress. Until we can step back and think, we're no good to ourselves or to anybody else. This will become more evident as we go forward, for we begin to see that hurting ourselves and others is fruitless. Other people suffer pain and are emotionally and spiritually ill, just as we are, and they deserve our compassion, just as we deserve it for ourselves.

This change in our outlook will take time. We can't let go of our old ways of thinking all at once. As with drinking and drugging, our obsession was lifted miraculously, by the grace of God, and this attitude shift, too, will come. Be kind and good to yourself.

When we do our daily inventory, we see where we have acted out our shortcomings. We examine our motives in each misplaced thought and action. We're learning to understand ourselves. We learn to visualize how we can right our wrongs, then do it. And we ask the God of our understanding to help us carry this information into tomorrow. Learning each day to admit and correct our shortcomings is our responsibility. This is how we become effective in our daily lives. This is character building.

This work with Step Ten will continue for the rest of our lives. During the day we "spot check" ourselves and notice what's bothering us, and address it thoughtfully, so as not to ruin the rest of our day. In the past we might have reacted impulsively or aggressively, but now we ask for a new approach. We thank the God of our understanding for the chance to make progress. With proper use of our will and the work we've done on ourselves, we gain sanity and serenity. We become loving and tolerant. We ask our God to direct our thinking and to remove from us the self-pity and grandiosity that only causes us far greater misery. Every day is a day to learn about God's will for us.

Suggested Directions for Step Ten

On page 112 of this book you will find a Suggested Daily Inventory Guide for Step Ten. The left-hand column lists the personality characteristics of a self-willed person. The right-hand column lists the personality characteristics of a God-willed individual, the person we seek to become. All we are trying to do is to get from the left-hand column to the right-hand column, not overnight but over time. Again, we seek not perfection but progress.

Suggested Daily Inventory Guide

Before we retire at night, we review our day and look at where we were resentful, dishonest, selfish, inconsiderate, or afraid. Did our qualities reflect self-will or following God's will? Use these lists to consider.

If we are guided by self-will, we are likely to be	**If we are guided by God's will, we are likely to be**
selfish and self-seeking	interested in others
dishonest	honest
inconsiderate	considerate
prideful	humble
greedy	giving or sharing
lustful	other-focused
angry	calm
envious	grateful
slothful	active
gluttonous	moderate
impatient	patient
intolerant	tolerant
resentful	forgiving
hateful	loving/concerned
harmful to others	doing good
self-pitying	self-forgetful
self-justifying	God-seeking
self-important	modest
suspicious	trusting
doubtful	faithful

At the end of each day, reflect on these lists for a few minutes. This practice can show us where we were today and what we want to continue to work on, bringing us to ask our Higher Power to help us in these areas. We slowly continue our spiritual growth. We ask for guidance and willingness to take inventory so as not to get filled up again with the parts of ourselves we find objectionable. We ask God to help us face and be rid of our self-centeredness.

We may also do an inventory specifically for our mental health and well-being by taking some time to reflect on the following questions:

- What were my external and internal triggers?
- How did I feel and act when I wasn't doing well?
- Was I symptomatic? If so, how did I feel and behave?
- What did I do to make myself feel better? What can I do in the future?

It might help to keep a daily journal and write your answers down, especially on difficult days.

There may be days when we need to use an additional strategy that lets us nurture ourselves and avoid stress-increasing activities. To further maintain our well-being, we make another list where we describe our physical and mental state when we feel well. Are we outgoing, active, caring, and friendly? We take the time to write about ourselves in as much detail as we can and try to get at all aspects of what being well feels like. On another sheet of paper, we then make a list of the things we need to do for ourselves every day to make ourselves feel okay. Following are some examples, but you'll decide what works for you: take a walk; take your medication; avoid caffeine, sugar, alcohol, or street drugs; find things you enjoy doing. Or perhaps just check in with yourself and with your Higher Power. This plan is for each of us to develop as a unique individual. Make your own list and try to follow it. Your list will likely change over time, and that's good; it's not to be written in stone. As you grow and heal and learn more about yourself, your strategies for maintaining your well-being will evolve.

It may also be helpful to review the mental symptoms inventory you did for Step Four. You can update your plan on days that are especially difficult to strengthen your well-being. Remember that it's important to give yourself permission to nurture yourself, to get validation from someone, and to pray or meditate. The purpose of your plan is to help you change, to the best of your ability in the moment, the negative thoughts to positive. As you try out your plan in actual trigger situations, you will begin to learn what works and what doesn't. With this new knowledge, go back and cross out those ideas that weren't effective. Continue to revise your plan as you learn more and more about yourself. When you have difficulty making your plan work for you, take in a meeting, share about it, start writing a journal about your experiences, go for a walk, listen to music, or do whatever you can do for yourself to relax enough to be able to work with these external circumstances.

Not everything that triggers us comes from outside ourselves, however. The other part of our mental health triggers can come from the inside and not be related to any stressful situation at all. Learning to identify our early warning signs can help us become more aware of internal triggers and allow us to take action before we drink or drug or wind up in the hospital. Some of the warning signs may be nervousness, lack of energy, isolating, having irrational thought patterns, erratic behavior, overeating, feeling frustrated or resentful, or obsessing about drinking or drugging. The list could go on. When any of these signs appear, we reach out for help, whether we want to in the moment or not. Reach out to someone—your sponsor, a friend, a service coordinator, any supportive person who is willing to listen and to share advice on what to do. Remember, it takes action on your part. At times of stress, do the things you have learned help you to relax; do something soothing for yourself. Give yourself permission to know that the things you are going to do for yourself feel right for you and are okay. But whatever else you do, call your sponsor or someone else in the fellowship before you pick up that drink or drug. Remember to surround yourself with affirming and loving people and be good to yourself. Take care of yourself and know that when things get difficult, *this too shall pass*.

Relevant Quote for Step Ten

"We will intuitively know how to handle situations that used to baffle us. We will suddenly realize that God is doing for us what we could not do for ourselves." (Big Book, p. 84)

Suggested Questions for Step Ten

1. How does taking a personal inventory help you grow spiritually?
2. When you find you were wrong, how do you go about admitting it?
3. How does promptly admitting being wrong set you free?
4. How can working on the Suggested Daily Inventory Guide help you in your recovery?

Step Eleven

Sought through prayer and meditation to improve our conscious contact with God as we understood Him, praying only for knowledge of His will for us and the power to carry that out.

Sometimes we may have used prayer and meditation to show ourselves as special above everyone. This is not spirituality; this is ego. The Eleventh Step, however, provides us with a spiritual foundation based on humility and service that furthers our recovery and leads us toward a life of peace and joy. Doing Step Eleven regularly helps us to improve our conscious contact with the God of our understanding and to know His will for us. The more we improve our conscious contact with God, the more important prayer and meditation become. It is easy to let go of our program of action and to fall back into old thinking and behaviors. What we really have in recovery is a daily reprieve, one day at a time, based on maintenance of our spiritual condition. Practicing the Eleventh Step keeps us spiritually fit and living in accord with what God wants for our lives. And so we make the decision to turn our wills and our lives over to the care of God as we understand Him.

Prayer and meditation are difficult for many of us. We might not believe in these things at all. Some of us may not have God as our Higher Power. Some of us saw no evidence of a God who cared in the lives we were leading. It was hard for many of us in the beginning to have a Higher Power to believe in and to pray to. But by practicing the Second Step, we gradually came to believe in a Power greater than ourselves whom we could trust and rely on. We might have begun praying by seeking only what God could do for us. "God, give me this" and "God, give me that." We gradually learned to focus our prayers on how we could best serve Him—Thy will, not ours, be done. Remember: doing the will of God is mainly being empowered to live the Twelve Steps, to love neighbor and self, and not to be mistaken in our idea of God and His will that comes not from our relationship with Him but from our mental disorder. Some of us, after all, were addicted to altered states; many of us used drugs and alcohol to achieve this.

In practicing the Eleventh Step we are developing the discipline of letting go of selfish attachments by praying for our fellows. When we were drinking and drugging and sought altered states, not taking care of our mental health, our self-will ran rampant, out of control. Now, our sole focus is in getting in touch with our Higher Power and understanding and living His will for us.

Each time we try to pray and meditate, we are brought a little closer to our Higher Power. The more we practice, the more certain we become of His presence, which is love. The power to love self and neighbor is a measure of His presence. Every opportunity we have to show kindness, love, and forgiveness can open our hearts and deepen our conscious contact with God, praying only for His will for us and for the power to carry it out. Spiritual life is not a theory. We must live it. It is real—concrete love of self and others as manifested, for example, in Twelfth Step work. We are gaining spiritual experience as we go. This is a gradual process; it is not easy but it is worth it.

We begin with the nightly inventory discussed in Step Ten. It is a tool for us to stay spiritually fit. We take a little quiet time with the God of our understanding. We may say something like: "God grant me the honesty, open mindedness, and willingness to accept your will, which is love, and give me the power to carry that out in these areas of self." We ask for guidance and strength, and to gain the ability to have the personality characteristics of someone with God's will in mind, not our own.

As we review our day every night, we also plan the day ahead every morning. We ask the God of our understanding to direct our hearts and minds with love. We are not perfect.

Resentments, fear, anger, and self-pity will come up. Humbly, we know we make mistakes and are spiritually ignorant, self-willed, and selfish. But we continue to right our wrongs as we go along; we have been given a set of tools to help us as we ask for inspiration and guidance. When we are upset or doubtful, we pause and ask for guidance and strength. We stop to ask of everything we do, "Is this loving, honest, and kind?" We stop fighting anything and anyone and look to help another person instead of focusing on ourselves. We have been given a new attitude and, for us, this is a miracle. As we grow, we develop a sixth sense of what is kind and truthful. It becomes an intuitive part of us. We become more experienced, and we know what to do in situations that earlier might have baffled us. We have learned to let go and enter the world of the spirit.

Meditation is quiet time without words to become centered, physically relaxed, and emotionally calm. It is an experience quite difficult to explain in words. It is hard for some people to begin to meditate. We each need to find our own way. Eventually, we do. What works for one person might not necessarily work for someone else. The purpose of meditation is to quiet the mind and to rejuvenate the spirit and be in contact with the body.

Meditation is a new skill for us; it takes time to learn. We are learning this new skill and practicing a new attitude in order to have a new understanding of His will for us. There are hundreds of different kinds of meditation practices. Choose one that makes you feel solid and real and peaceful. Prayer helps increase our conscious contact with our Higher Power; meditation helps us to grow spiritually. Our will becomes aligned with God's will for us.

As you practice Step Eleven, your relationship with your Higher Power becomes the most important relationship in your life, that from which all other relationships can grow. All relationships need to be nurtured with special times put aside; the relationship with your Higher Power is no different. So, as it has been suggested, upon awakening in the morning and before we retire at night, we learn to pray and meditate, nurturing and developing our relationship with the God of our understanding. We have come to experience belonging; our world is no longer as hostile as it was before; we have found purpose and meaning. It is now time for us to move on to the Twelfth Step.

Suggested Directions for Step Eleven

Those of us wondering how to begin to meditate might want to look at *Twelve Steps and Twelve Traditions* (the "Twelve and Twelve") for suggestions, beginning with the prayer of St. Francis of Assisi quoted on page 99: "Lord, make me a channel of Thy peace—that where there is hatred, I may bring love—that where there is wrong, I may bring the spirit of forgiveness—that where there is discord, I may bring harmony—that where there is error, I may bring truth—that where there is doubt, I may bring faith—that where there is despair, I may bring hope—that where there are shadows, I may bring light—that where there is sadness, I may bring joy. Lord, grant that I may seek rather to comfort than to be comforted—to understand, than to be understood—to love, than to be loved. For it is by self-forgetting that one finds. It is by forgiving that one is forgiven. It is by dying that one awakens to Eternal Life. Amen."

The passage continues, "As beginners in meditation, we might now reread this prayer several times very slowly, savoring every word and trying to take in the deep meaning of each phrase and idea. It will help if we can drop all resistance to what our friend says. For in meditation, debate has no place. We rest quietly with the thoughts of someone who knows, so that we may experience and learn."

Relevant Quotes for Step Eleven

On God: "We well remember how something deep inside us kept rebelling against the idea of bowing before any God. Many of us had strong logic, too, which 'proved' there was no God whatsoever. What about all the accidents, sickness, cruelty, and injustice in the world? What about all these unhappy lives which were the direct result of unfortunate birth and uncontrollable circumstances? Surely there could be no justice in this scheme of things, and therefore no God at all." (Twelve and Twelve, pp. 96–97)

On what we pray for: "We ask especially for freedom from self-will, and are careful to make no requests for ourselves only. We may ask for ourselves, however, if others will be helped. We are careful never to pray for our own selfish ends." (Big Book, p. 87)

Starting each day: "On awakening let us think about the twenty-four hours ahead. We consider our plans for the day. Before we begin, we ask God to direct our thinking, especially asking that it be divorced from self-pity, dishonest or self-seeking motives. Under these conditions we can employ our mental faculties with assurance, for after all God gave us brains to use. Our thought-life will be placed on a much higher plane when our thinking is cleared of wrong motives." (Big Book, p. 86)

Suggested Questions for Step Eleven

1. What blocks you from seeking to improve conscious contact with the God of your understanding?
2. What does it mean to you to pray for the knowledge of God's will for you and the power to carry it out?
3. Describe a situation where you had knowledge of God's will to be kind and honest but you were not. What happened?

4. Make a list of all the feelings and thoughts you falsely believe are spiritual that happen when your mental disorder takes over, often after you are triggered. These feelings and thoughts are to be viewed as danger signs. Your spiritual task in part is overcoming them.

5. What real, concrete spiritual experience of loving kindness can disarm or replace the danger signs?

Step Twelve

Having had a spiritual awakening as a result of these Steps, we tried to carry this message to other dually diagnosed people, and to practice these principles in all our affairs.

As we continue to work our program of action in the Twelfth Step, we reach out to help our fellow dually diagnosed brothers and sisters who still suffer, sharing with them what we have been given. Nothing will help us more than giving away what our program has given us. Our lives take on new meaning as we watch other people recover and as we see our fellowship growing around us. The Twelfth Step is about sharing with others the gifts of wellness through a spirit of service. This is our gift from God. The strength of a Double Trouble in Recovery group lies in the desire of its members to share, with other DTR members, their stories and the Steps taken to gain and maintain recovery. We nurture our spirit by helping other dually diagnosed members, thus ensuring the growth of our fellowship. We carry the message of recovery from mental disorders and substance abuse to others who suffer because it helps us to stay clean and sober ourselves, and it boosts our own mental well-being.

All we want to do is be helpful. People do recover from mental disorders and substance abuse: this is a principle of faith. But we have learned that trying to persuade someone to follow our way is a waste of time. Still, we are present for others and willing to help because we remember when we were as they are now. We remember what it took for us to hear the message of recovery. We put ourselves in others' place and ask ourselves how we would like to be approached. We try our best to walk in others' shoes. We do not force ourselves on anybody because we might ruin the opportunity of being helpful at some other time.

In carrying our message, we allow others the right to be wrong. We are careful not to identify anyone as dually diagnosed. We allow people to draw their own conclusions. We do not play God. We simply share our own experiences with those who are willing to listen. We tell them about the hopelessness and helplessness we have suffered, and we humbly offer a solution by describing our experience with our program of action and faith. We never put a newcomer down. We talk about what works for us. We offer friendship and fellowship.

Don't be discouraged if newcomers don't respond as you want them to. You are not responsible for the choices of another. We take on the responsibility of reaching out to others because that is essential to our own recovery. This type of giving is itself our reward, and we expect nothing in return. Our brothers and sisters who seek a new beginning at DTR might still be in trouble when they come to the program. There will be no greater joy and happiness than to watch them awaken to the presence of a loving God of their understanding, bringing their lives new purpose and meaning. That is a job well done.

We may see our fellows "slip"—briefly use substances again—or even relapse into habitual use. If so, we may be deeply discouraged about our ability to carry the message. But that feeling is misplaced. Please believe that by the grace of God we have only been asked to help; it is not up to us whether our efforts will actually bring another dually diagnosed person into recovery. For whatever reason, the God of our understanding has laid out some other plan for some of us. Ours is only to help them as calmly as we can by carrying the message.

DTR members suffer from anxiety, depression, or other mental health disorders, and these conditions may play a part in our slips. In fact, they can feel overwhelming. Some of us may be suffering from a personal calamity and slip when we can't find the resources to face it. Don't be discouraged. We've all learned the hard way that one drink or drug can start the cycle all over again, but it doesn't have to. A slip can be overcome. Ask those who have slipped if they are placing recovery first. Ask if they are asking for guidance from their

Higher Power and listening for answers. We have found that a dependence upon Him for forgiveness is humbling as well as uplifting and works when nothing else does. With this attitude we will not be shaken by others' challenges, and we can be helpful messengers of the DTR principles and practices. We have also seen our fellows stay clean and sober, and we have seen what it takes.

We all deserve a chance. No one is better or worse than anyone else in DTR. Each of us deserves that opportunity to recover. When any brother or sister reaches out a hand for help, our hearts will be open to them and we will lend a hand on the road to recovery. There is always an available chair at our meetings for anyone with a desire to recover. When someone in our group relapses into substance use, or neglects his or her mental health needs, it is not our fault. We don't have that kind of power. A relapse—if the person survives it—may lead to the awakening necessary for that person to finally take action and commit to the Twelve Step recovery journey.

With Step Twelve, we've found a common solution and we're ready to join our brothers and sisters in recovery in carrying this message to others. We tell of what brought us to the program and what has changed in our lives; we stress the spiritual part of Double Trouble in Recovery. Having suffered, we understand the illness and know that we have experienced grace. We listen, share our personal experience, and pray for others. We know gratitude for our own recovery best when we carry the message to others. Without active service, we move backwards; gratitude is then only a vague feeling. To bring it to life, we must act on it.

When sharing with a new member just coming into DTR, we see our pasts looking us straight in the face; we see the pain and confusion we knew. We look into their hopeful eyes and extend our hands to them and know that miracles can happen, because they happened for us. We have found a new freedom, freedom from the bondage of self. Our lives have become manageable and, with God's help, we can show this new freedom to other dually diagnosed people. We can show others that they too can get over their fears and their sufferings—and replace them with faith.

In what way have we been made ready to receive this gift and to practice all of the Twelve Steps of our program? Many of us might puzzle over this "spiritual awakening"; we may look for something dramatic to happen to us, like a lightning strike. But in fact, our experience evolves from within. We gain our new way of thinking and acting from practicing the Steps. It happens slowly, over time. But eventually we come to see that something new and different has happened to us, something we couldn't have believed possible in the past. This "something" is the spiritual awakening, the release from the bondage of self. It's a new closeness to the God of our understanding. It's a new consciousness, the result of our working the Twelve Steps of our program. We've been restored to faith and hope, to honesty, open-minded willingness, and to a newfound strength. We are on a new journey. We have found a set of tools that has transformed our past into a source of strength, honesty, forgiveness, tolerance, love, and understanding. In the past, these feelings were alien to us. Now, they are our gifts. But we had to prepare ourselves to receive them, and we gained that readiness through our practice of the Twelve Steps. Our task is to be an example to others, a living testimony that our program works if we work it.

We work the program by practicing its principles in all of our affairs. This is a small statement, but it's a big order. We practice to the best of our ability. We acknowledge that we're not perfect, but that's no excuse for not making the effort. We learn to apply the principles in different areas of our lives daily. By praying for an open mind and a new journey, we can see that our old ways of living could be replaced with the spiritual principles of the Twelve Steps. Can we accept this responsibility? Can we come to terms with the mental disorders from which we suffer? Can we accept who we are with courage and serenity? Can we deal with boredom and pain by practicing the Steps in all our affairs? Yes, we can, if we are sincere in our efforts. We will fall short at times even though we are not drinking and drugging, but we can find the resources to rise above our failings and meet life's challenges as they come. Can we turn these challenges into opportunities for growth and become more comfortable with them? If we are willing to live a program of action and to have faith in a Higher Power who can sustain us through any difficulty, we take whatever troubles we must face and turn them into demonstrations of faith. In meetings we see other dually diagnosed people successfully dealing with problems of mental disorders and substance abuse, meeting life on its own terms. We will continue to be faced with life's challenges. Our answer is still more spiritual development.

Upon embarking on our journey of recovery, we first admitted powerlessness over our addiction and our mental disorders; we saw how unmanageable our lives had become. Until we admitted our powerlessness over drugs and alcohol and over our mental disorders, we could not see ourselves. We had no awareness of our compulsion, craving, and obsession to use. We had no understanding of the spiritual malady from which we suffered. We could not rid ourselves of our problems; we continued to use and were unable to work on our mental health.

We came to see in Step One a new beginning on a path of recovery. We were awakened as a result of Step One. We became able to admit that we had a problem, and though it took tremendous effort to admit our own truth, this truth gave us the strength to start practicing the spiritual principle of honesty. We found a sense of humility we could not have gained on our own.

In Step Two, we looked at a Power greater than ourselves who could restore us to sanity; we came to believe that the obsession to use could and would be lifted from us.

We were still dually diagnosed, but we didn't have to fight anymore. We were granted the spiritual gift of hope to go on, one day at a time.

In Step Three we made a decision to turn our will and our lives over to the care of God as we understood Him. We wanted to change and not return to drugs and alcohol. We wanted to take care of our mental health. We had the willingness to believe in a Power greater than ourselves, and we chose our own conception of God.

In Steps Four and Five we searched fearlessly for the truth about ourselves. We found that doing our inventory alone wasn't enough, we needed to share our truth with God and another human being in honesty, asking God to remove the character defects blocking us from living the lives we so desperately needed and wanted. So we found the courage to share the exact nature of our wrongs with God and with someone we trusted. We found the spiritual principle of integrity. But that was still not enough. We had to go further with more action. Not only did we want freedom from our misery, we wanted to learn to accept life on life's terms. This was an essential part of our spiritual awakening.

We had a choice. We could either accept it, or we could stay miserable. Many of us balked at Step Six because we were not entirely ready for God to remove our character defects. It took willingness on our parts to put the defects of character on paper and sit with them. Even if they were killing us, we had a hard time letting them go!

We came to terms with the fact that we still had flaws of character that we couldn't give up yet. We said to ourselves, "This perhaps I cannot do today, but I can stop saying never." Then in Step Seven we humbly asked God to remove our shortcomings. In Step Eight we continued our housecleaning for we saw our conflicts not only with ourselves, but also with people and situations in the world in which we lived. We had to begin to make peace. So we became willing to set things right. We followed this up in Step Nine by making direct amends to those concerned, except when doing so would injure them or others.

By Step Ten we had begun to establish a basis for our daily living. We realized that we would need to continue taking personal inventory and that when we were wrong we ought to admit it promptly. In Step Eleven we saw that if a Higher Power had restored us to sanity and enabled us to live with some peace of mind in a surely troubled world, then such a Higher Power was worth knowing better by as direct a contact as possible. We found that the consistent use of meditation and prayer opened the path to our Higher Power. Where there had once been a trickle there was now a river of love and guidance from God, which would only grow as we were better able to understand His will for us.

We will never forget those days of unhappiness and unrest when we were the newcomers in DTR. We have learned to change resentment into acceptance, fear into hope, and anger into love. Now, with Step Twelve, we are ready to help others, and in so doing, to help ourselves. When we persistently do this, our program of attraction will bring many newcomers.

Relevant Quotes for Step Twelve

We are reborn: "When, with God's help, we calmly accepted our lot, then we found we could live at peace with ourselves and show others who still suffered the same fears that they could get over them, too. We found that freedom from fear was more important than freedom from want." (Twelve and Twelve, p. 122)

"As we grow spiritually, we find that our old attitudes toward our instincts need to undergo drastic revisions. Our desires for emotional security and wealth, for personal prestige and power, for romance, and for family satisfactions—all these have to be tempered and redirected. We have learned that the satisfaction of instincts cannot be the sole end and aim of our lives . . . when we are willing to place spiritual growth first—then and only then do we have a real chance." (Twelve and Twelve, p. 114)

God bless: "Our book is meant to be suggestive only. We realize we know only a little. God will constantly disclose more to you and to us. Ask him in your morning meditation what you can do each day for the man who is still sick. The answer will come if your own house is in order . . . Abandon yourself to God as you understand God. Admit your faults to Him and to your fellows. Clear away the wreckage of your past. Give freely of what you find and join us. We shall be with you in the Fellowship of the Spirit, and you will surely meet some of us as you trudge the Road of Happy Destiny.

"May God bless you and keep you—until then." (Big Book, p. 164)

Suggested Questions for Step Twelve

1. How has your life changed as a result of working the Twelfth Step?
2. How are you carrying the message to other dually diagnosed people?
3. How do you practice the principles of the Steps in all of your affairs?
4. What has been most difficult for you in working the Twelfth Step?

The Twelve Traditions of Double Trouble in Recovery

1. Our common welfare should come first; personal recovery depends on DTR unity.
2. For our group purpose, there is but one ultimate authority—a loving God as He may express Himself in our group conscience. Our leaders are but trusted servants; they do not govern.
3. The only requirement for DTR membership is a desire to stop drinking and drugging, and to work on one's mental health.
4. Each group should be autonomous except in matters affecting other groups or Double Trouble in Recovery as a whole.
5. Each group has but one primary purpose—to carry its message to the dually diagnosed person who still suffers.
6. A Double Trouble in Recovery group ought never endorse, finance, or lend the DTR name to any related facility or outside enterprise,

lest problems of money, property, and prestige divert us from our primary purpose.

7. Every Double Trouble in Recovery group ought to be self-supporting, declining outside contributions.

8. Double Trouble in Recovery should remain forever nonprofessional, but our service centers may employ special workers.

9. Double Trouble in Recovery, as such, ought never be organized; but we may create service boards or committees directly responsible to those they serve.

10. Double Trouble in Recovery has no opinion on outside issues; hence the DTR name ought never be drawn into public controversy.

11. Our public relations policy is based on attraction rather than promotion; we need always maintain personal anonymity at the level of press, radio, and films.

12. Anonymity is the spiritual foundation of all our traditions, ever reminding us to place principles before personalities.

The Twelve Traditions are adapted with permission of Alcoholics Anonymous World Services, Inc. Permission to reprint and adapt the Twelve Traditions does not mean that AA is in any way affiliated with this program. AA is a program of recovery from alcoholism—use of the Twelve Traditions in connection with programs and activities that are patterned after AA but address other problems does not imply otherwise.

Tradition One

Our common welfare should come first; personal recovery depends on DTR unity.

The DTR fellowship's common welfare is our first concern. Each member is a part of the group; our own interests are inseparable from the broader integrity of the group. Our own road to recovery depends on spiritual principles, and on the conscience of the group. As we look more closely at these facts, the realization dawns on us that we are a small part of a great whole. As painful as that ego deflation may be, recovery is what takes its place. We learn to live and work and love together, and the continuation of Double Trouble is the primary reason for the group. It's a wonderful new experience. By faith and work, we will learn the lessons necessary to increase and sustain the unity of our program. Hence our common welfare will come first, and personal recovery depends upon Double Trouble unity.

Tradition Two

For our group purpose, there is but one ultimate author-ity—a loving God as He may express Himself in our group conscience. Our leaders are but trusted servants; they do not govern.

Those of us who become members of the DTR fellowship become the voice of the group conscience. It is wiser than any single leader could be. All individuals need to be heard, but the group conscience is the decision maker; the ultimate authority is a loving God as He may express Himself in our group conscience. It's our responsibility to discover and express that group conscience as we elect chairpersons and treasurers, pass the hat, and conduct other business. There is no absolute authority beyond a loving God. This takes the control out of any one person's hands and places it squarely in the hands of the group collectively.

Tradition Three

The only requirement for DTR membership is a desire to stop drinking and drugging, and to work on one's mental health.

Our membership includes all of us who have a mental disorder and a substance abuse problem, no matter how low we have gone, no matter how grave our complications. Even our crimes cannot deny us membership or keep us out. With our desire to stop using and to work on our mental health, we meet our sole requirement. We all have the same chance at recovery. We have no membership regulations. Newcomers decide for themselves if they should join. We never force anyone to believe anything, conform to anything, or contribute funds. As we were freely given the grace to recover, so shall anyone who crosses our threshold be given assistance freely.

Tradition Four

Each group should be autonomous except in matters affecting other groups or Double Trouble in Recovery as a whole.

Each group will manage its own affairs, except when the DTR fellowship as a whole is affected. The group is responsible to no authority other than its own conscience, except when its plans may have implications for other groups as well. Then, those groups ought to be consulted. No group, regional committee, or individual should ever take any action that might greatly affect DTR as a whole without conferring with the trustees of the DTR board on such issues. Our common welfare comes first.

Remember that every group starts with two or three dually diagnosed people gathered together for recovery. They can call themselves a Double Trouble in Recovery group provided that as a group, they have no other affiliation and are not run by professionals. A group starts when someone makes the effort to gather others together for this purpose. There is no other way. After the group has started, the original leaders have to foster a sense of democracy, which springs up from the grassroots. This democracy will eventually replace the original leadership, which is as it should be. As that happens, the group declares itself strictly reliant on its own conscience as a guide to action. A group should not do anything that will injure DTR as a whole. It should not affiliate itself with anything or anybody else. Recovery from mental disorders and substance abuse has to be its sole purpose.

We elect new trusted servants by majority vote, and all plans for group action have to be approved by the majority. This means no single individual can appoint himself or herself to act for the group as a whole.

Let us remember that any group of men and women that cannot correct its own faults will fail. Grow or fail—that's the rule. Just as members take their own inventories and act on them, so must our whole group. If we are to survive and to serve usefully, we must take our own inventory as a group.

It's been proven that DTR can stand on its own feet under any conditions. It has to outgrow dependence on the professional community that helped it begin. It should outgrow dependence on the efforts of the older members, too. New, able, and vigorous people keep turning up where they are needed because DTR has reached enough spiritual maturity to know that its final dependence is upon God.

Tradition Five

Each group has but one primary purpose—to carry its message to the dually diagnosed person who still suffers.

Each group ought to be a spiritual entity, having one primary purpose—carrying its message to persons who still suffer from mental disorders and substance abuse. Unless we carry the message, we ourselves cannot recover and stay recovered from the spiritual malady of mind and body. And unless we carry the message, we won't reach those who haven't yet sat in the chairs in our group circle.

Faith is our greatest gift; sharing with others is our greatest responsibility. May we continually seek the honesty, open-mindedness, and willingness that manifests in the truth of our experience, both before we came to the group and now. May we fulfill the immense trust that has been placed in our hands. No satisfaction is greater and no joy deeper than carrying the message to a person who still suffers. To be able to share in the miracle of watching men and women open their eyes with wonder as they move from darkness into light, to see their lives fill with purpose and meaning, and above all to watch them awaken to the presence of a loving God in their lives—this is what we receive as we carry the message.

Our primary purpose is to think of those still to come to DTR as they try to return to faith and to life. We want them to find everything that we have found and more, if that be possible. We have come to realize how little we know, and how much more will be revealed by our Higher Power. Ask in your morning meditation what you can do each day for the man or woman who is still suffering; the answer will come if your own house is in order. It sounds like a big order. Easy does it. Obviously, to carry this message, we ourselves must be clear. See to it that your relationship with your Higher Power is right, and great events will come to pass for you and for many others.

Tradition Six

*A Double Trouble in Recovery group ought never endorse,
finance, or lend the DTR name to any related facility or
outside enterprise, lest problems of money, property, and
prestige divert us from our primary purpose.*

Problems of money, property, and authority may easily
divert us from our primary spiritual aim. Therefore, any
property to be used specifically for DTR (such as renting a
room in a church or other building, or a free-standing clubhouse) should be separately incorporated and managed, thus
separating the material from the spiritual. A DTR group, as
such, should never go into business. Mental health facilities
or hospitals or clubs ought not to have the use of the DTR
name given to them. Their management should be the sole
responsibility of those people who financially support them.
If members have secured and are able to support a separate
clubhouse, DTR members may be preferred as managers or
employees. While a DTR group may cooperate with anyone, such cooperation ought never to go so far as affiliation

or endorsement, actual or implied. A DTR group can bind itself to no one.

Tradition Seven

Every Double Trouble in Recovery group ought to be self-supporting, declining outside contributions.

Probably no DTR tradition at this present time in our growth is more painful. Each group ought to be self-supporting by voluntary contributions of its own members. We need to recognize that for DTR to function, each member should regularly contribute to the facility, the meeting place, the clubhouse, the hospital that lends us a meeting room, even if the amount is only a dollar. Most groups pass a hat at each meeting for this purpose, but unfortunately some of us hesitate to chip in. We are quite tight with our money; some of us live on a fixed income. But we are not asking for money to make ourselves rich. We are simply trying to keep our groups self-supporting so that they are autonomous, unbeholden to any outside donors. Any public solicitation of funds using the DTR name is highly dangerous, whether by clubs, groups, or other outside agencies. Acceptance of large gifts from any source carrying any obligation whatsoever is unwise. Experience has shown us that nothing could destroy us more than disputes over property, money, or authority.

Each group can find its own ways to inspire its members to support it financially. Whatever way your group can do that, please do so for the safety and future of your group. Keeping your group self-sufficient will keep the focus on spirituality.

Tradition Eight

Double Trouble in Recovery should remain forever non-professional, but our service centers may employ special workers.

DTR should remain nonprofessional. Many of us have struggled through the mental health community, and some of us have successfully become peer specialists or service providers within that system. Others have gone back to school in one form or another and become professionals in our own right. This is good. However, DTR should never have a professional class. In a DTR group, all members should be on equal footing—even if some members also hold jobs as counselors, for example. Our mutual support operates in a realm different from the professional realm, with its hierarchy, degrees, and compensation. Carrying the DTR message and doing service must remain a grassroots effort, linking dually diagnosed people to each other. This service is a key ingredient of our recovery program. Our program must be free to be effective. Freely we have received, and freely shall we give.

There is, however, a great need for fellowship members to assume the responsibilities associated with the administration and the everyday management of DTR and its groups as well as assisting other members as they learn to navigate the mental health system and gain independence in the recovery community. These duties would otherwise be fulfilled by persons not dually diagnosed. Rather than service, these duties fall within the confines of administration or clinical work. In these capacities, members can and should receive compensation without detriment to themselves, others, or to the fellowship. Thus, such duties as maintaining DTR meeting sites, answering phones, or coordinating meetings regionally can be compensated.

In sum, our Twelfth Step is never to be paid, as it is its own reward. But those who labor in our community mental health system and other areas should always receive fair compensation for their work.

Tradition Nine

Double Trouble in Recovery, as such, ought never be organized; but we may create service boards or committees directly responsible to those they serve.

Double Trouble in Recovery groups are democratic, grassroots organizations. Hierarchies do not suit the spirit of DTR. When it comes to organized leadership, less is better. Rotating leadership is the best. The small group may elect its secretary and chairperson, the large group its rotating committee, and the groups of a large metropolitan area their central or integral committee, which may employ a full-time secretary. Like Alcoholics Anonymous, DTR may one day have a General Service Committee to serve as custodians of our DTR Traditions and to be the recipients of voluntary DTR contributions by which we will be able to maintain a DTR General Service Office. They will be authorized to handle our overall public relations and guarantee the integrity of our work. All such representatives are to be guided by the spirit of service. For true members of DTR are but trusted and experienced servants of the whole. They derive no real authority from their title; they do not govern. Universal respect is the key to their usefulness.

Tradition Ten

Double Trouble in Recovery has no opinion on outside issues; hence the DTR name ought never be drawn into public controversy.

No DTR group or member should express on behalf of the fellowship any opinion on outside issues. DTR should never be implicated or take a position on any such issues, particularly those of politics, mental health reform, medication, alcoholism, or sectarian religion. We oppose no one in the name of DTR; therefore, we express no group views. We focus solely on our own recovery. As a fellowship, we do not enter into public controversy, for we will perish if we do. The survival of DTR and spreading our message is of far greater importance than any other cause. Since recovery from dual diagnosis is life itself to us, we put all our means of strength into that survival. For our own sake, we learn to work together, to live together, and to make DTR more effective to do the most good for those dually diagnosed. We learn from our predecessor, AA, and its humble beginnings, to keep our society out of public controversy. Outside issues are simply not our focus.

Tradition Eleven

Our public relations policy is based on attraction rather than promotion; we need always maintain personal anonymity at the level of press, radio, and films.

The DTR fellowship started by word of mouth, bringing together dually diagnosed fellows from hospitals, prisons, day treatment programs, institutions, and homelessness. Family members helped spread the word too. But our growth wasn't by word of mouth alone. Without help from the community mental health system, the fellowship could never have grown as it has. Many of us have come to DTR through such channels. Doctors, social workers, and counselors read about DTR and called for more information. Articles were written and inquiries made. Therefore, a great responsibility falls upon us to develop the best possible public relations policy for DTR. Like many other fellowships, we have come to rely mostly on the principle of attraction rather than promotion and to choose anonymity when dealing with the public.

Promotion and attraction are two contrasting ideas. Many organizations promote and advertise their virtues, drawing attention to themselves in order to obtain new business or funding. Attraction, on the other hand, starts with the person receiving the message and happens only if the message is relevant to that individual. DTR's public relations policy is based on attraction rather than promotion. We have nothing to sell; we live our spiritual program of recovery to the best of our ability and we attract by example. The message comes through us to others who are dually diagnosed: they may come to meetings and freely choose whether to embrace DTR as their program of recovery. If they identify with our stories and would like to have what we now have, then they are ready to join us on our path to recovery. That is the attraction on which DTR's public relations policy rests.

Our tradition of anonymity is shared with many other fellowships: we refer to ourselves and each other only by first name (and the initial of our last name if we wish). In doing so, we emphasize our equality as fellows in recovery, and we give up our natural desire for personal distinction as DTR members. As each of us takes part in this tradition, we weave a protective fence around our society when we grow and work in unity.

But anonymity is complicated by the fact that word about DTR spreads through non-anonymous channels, such as the mental health system and the media. We have learned in DTR that the public eye can be hazardous, especially for us. Yet it is necessary for some of us who speak in public to inform and educate about dual diagnosis. We have no fear to discuss this matter as long as we do not put our program in jeopardy. Clearly we need to publicize our work. Some DTR members may be in a position to do this, but letting our non-DTR friends in the system do this for us is a great help to our anonymity. To those of our friends who have written about us to make us known in the community, we thank you for carrying our message. We are more than a good story; we are miracles. But it is best to understand that if we refuse personally to go public because of our anonymity, it doesn't mean that we don't want to pass on the message. We want our message, our program, and its principles to be conveyed. But we wish to publicize its principles and its work without publicizing its individual members.

Tradition Twelve

Anonymity is the spiritual foundation of all our traditions,
ever reminding us to place principles before personalities.

Anonymity has an immense spiritual significance. It reminds us to place principles before personalities, to practice genuine humility, and to give up our personal gains for the common good of our fellowship. Keeping the spirit of anonymity means sacrificing one's desire for power, prestige, and money made through DTR or connections made in its fellowship. It must become a general practice in our fellowship lest our whole program be destroyed. Clearly, every member's name and story needs to be kept confidential if that person wishes for it to be so.

However, for those of us who work to lift the stigma of mental illness, we must ask, "How anonymous should our members be?" It is easy to argue that our disclosures help dispel the fears about mental disorders and substance abuse. Indeed, many people have been helped by those of us who have carried this message into our conversations outside the

DTR fellowship and in our education of the public. So it may seem that we wouldn't want to be too strict in preserving our anonymity. One could argue that the word-of-mouth method is limited, that our work needs to be publicized to reach those who need it. And after all, our work has received public approval and recognition in the community mental health system as well as in newspapers and magazine articles.

Still, we must think carefully before discussing DTR with mental health professionals or the media. It's essential that we know how this should be done: members must not present themselves as conveying "the" message. Whenever we speak of DTR outside of meetings, we are speaking for ourselves only and not for the whole fellowship. Anonymity protects more than our own identity; it also protects DTR from being identified with any single member. There is still a very fine line between doing great good and great harm. There have, for instance, been times when our trusted servants have gone back to drinking and drugging, and without their anonymity, the fellowship of DTR could suffer.

These experiences have taught us, therefore, that anonymity is really humility at work. It is a pervading spirituality that moves us, we hope, to give up our natural desire for personal distinction as DTR members, both before our fellows and the general public. We protect our anonymity in order to protect our fellowship. And we must protect our fellowship so it may grow and continue to help the dually diagnosed who still suffer from addiction and mental illness. And thus our anonymity is the greatest safeguard we can have.

Appendix A: Format and Script for DTR Meetings

Meeting Format

DTR meetings follow a traditional Twelve Step format. Most groups meet for sixty to ninety minutes. Following are the standard elements of a meeting.

Welcome

Before the meeting starts, the group leader (and any coleaders) meet and greet people as they come in. This helps to create a climate of warmth and hospitality.

Introduction

The group leader introduces himself or herself by first name only, welcomes everyone to the meeting, and discloses his or her dual diagnosis. At this point, it is especially important to welcome back people who have been absent, including those who have returned after a slip, a relapse, or a stay in a treatment center or hospital. These members are greeted with acceptance and nonjudgment.

Moment of Silence

The leader invites everyone to observe a moment of silent reflection for members who are absent, hospitalized, or experiencing other setbacks related to their substance use and mental disorders. The group is then invited to recite the Serenity Prayer.

Readings

The leader asks various members to read key statements about DTR, including

- the DTR Preamble
- "How It Works"
- the Twelve Steps of DTR
- "The Promises"
- "On Recovery"

These readings can be found in appendix B.

Group Member Introductions

Next, group members have an opportunity to introduce themselves, using their first names only, and to identify themselves as having a dual diagnosis. This step gives everyone a chance to be welcomed by the group and to feel accepted. Group members greet each self-introduction with a simple "Hi" or "Welcome."

Group Guidelines

The leader reminds members about the rules for behavior during the meeting:

- Members are not to bring alcohol, nonprescription drugs, or drug paraphernalia to meetings. This is to protect the group, the meeting place, and DTR as a whole.
- Members who have taken alcohol or nonprescription drugs in the last twenty-four hours are asked to refrain from sharing during the second part of the meeting. The leader suggests that these members speak to the group leader, to the guest speaker, or to another member at the end of the meeting.
- DTR is an anonymous program. What takes place during the meeting "stays in the room" when the meeting ends. The names of group members and what they said or did during the meeting remains confidential. This protects everyone and helps engender a feeling of trust and comfort in the group.
- Members are asked to limit their comments during the sharing time to five minutes. This

ensures that everyone has a chance to talk, and
that the meeting ends on time.

- After a member shares his or her feelings, there
is no cross-talk or lecturing of the person who
has spoken. Members are asked to talk only
about their own experiences as they relate to
the topic of the meeting.

- If the group needs to take up a collection to
pay small expenses associated with running the
group, members will "pass a basket" to collect
donations.

Guest Speaker

At some meetings, the leader sets aside fifteen to twenty
minutes for a speaker to share his or her experiences in dealing with dual diagnosis.

Sharing

If time permits, group members are invited to speak briefly
about their experiences. Again, sharing is voluntary, and
some people may choose to "pass."

Closing

To end the meeting, group members often recite the Serenity
Prayer as a group. Sometimes another moment of silence is
observed.

Meeting Script

Following is a "script" (based on the above guidelines) for DTR meeting leaders to use. It is written for a speaker meeting but can be adapted for any other meeting format.

> *Hi, my name is* (leader's first name), *and I am dually diagnosed. I'd like to welcome everyone to this meeting of Double Trouble in Recovery. We meet here* (give the scheduled day and time).

> *Please help me open this meeting with a moment of silence for those still sick and suffering dually diagnosed persons in and out of the room, followed by the Serenity Prayer for those who care to join me.* (The group recites the Serenity Prayer.)

> *I've asked* (first name) *to read the DTR Preamble.* (Reading follows.)

> *I've asked* (first name) *to read "How It Works" and the Twelve Steps of DTR.* (Reading follows.)

> *I've asked* (first name) *to read "The Promises."* (Reading follows.)

> *I've asked* (first name) *to read "On Recovery."* (Reading follows.)

I'd like to thank my readers.

Now I'd like to extend a warm welcome to any newcomers and anyone who's just coming back. Just sit, relax, and listen. Is this anyone's first meeting, or are there any newcomers? Would anyone like to introduce themselves? (Introductions follow.)

This is an anonymous program, which means that who you see here and what you hear here stays here in this room. This is so we all feel comfortable with what we say.

Our speaker (first name) *is here to share* (his/her) *experience, strength, and hope. When the speaker speaks, we suggest that you do not compare stories, but identify with the feelings. We all took different routes to get here, but the feelings are the same.* (Speaker follows.)

We will now open the meeting for sharing. We ask that you limit your sharing to five minutes to give everyone who wishes a chance to speak. (Sharing follows.)

Anonymity is the spiritual foundation of all traditions, ever reminding us to put principles before personalities. This means that who you see, what you hear—please leave it here when you leave.

We have a nice way of closing. Please join together in reciting the Serenity Prayer. (Recitation of the Serenity Prayer follows.)

Appendix B: Readings for DTR Meetings

The Serenity Prayer

God, grant me the serenity to accept the things
I cannot change,
courage to change the things I can,
and wisdom to know the difference.

DTR Preamble

Double Trouble in Recovery is a fellowship of men and women who share their experience, strength, and hope with each other so that they may solve their common problems and help others to recover from their particular addiction(s) and mental disorders.

Double Trouble in Recovery is designed to meet the needs of the dually diagnosed and is clearly for those having addictive substance problems as well as having been diagnosed with a mental disorder.

We also address the problems and benefits associated with psychiatric medication as well as other issues crucial to mental health; thus we recognize that for many, having addiction and mental disorders represents *Double Trouble in Recovery*.

There are no dues or fees for DTR membership; we are self-supporting through our own contributions.

Double Trouble in Recovery is not affiliated with any sect, denomination, political group, organization, or institution.

Our primary purpose is to maintain freedom from our addiction(s) and to maintain our well-being.

How It Works

We band together to help ourselves recover from our addictions and mental disorders. We share our experiences in order to help ourselves to become honest, open-minded, and willing. Sharing helps all of us to remember how it was and how we arrived at where we are today.

We live *one day at a time* and practice the Twelve Steps of DTR.

The Twelve Steps of Double Trouble in Recovery

1. We admitted we were powerless over our mental disorders and substance abuse—that our lives had become unmanageable.

2. Came to believe that a Power greater than ourselves could restore us to sanity.

3. Made a decision to turn our will and our lives over to the care of God *as we understood Him.*

4. Made a searching and fearless moral inventory of ourselves.

5. Admitted to God, to ourselves, and to another human being the exact nature of our wrongs.

6. Were entirely ready to have God remove all these defects of character.

7. Humbly asked Him to remove our shortcomings.

8. Made a list of all persons we had harmed, and became willing to make amends to them all.

9. Made direct amends to such people wherever possible, except when to do so would injure them or others.

10. Continued to take personal inventory and when we were wrong promptly admitted it.

11. Sought through prayer and meditation to improve our conscious contact with God *as we understood Him*, praying only for knowledge of His will for us and the power to carry that out.

12. Having had a spiritual awakening as the result of these Steps, we tried to carry this message to other dually diagnosed people, and to practice these principles in all our affairs.

The Promises

If we are painstaking about this phase of our development, we will be amazed before we are halfway through. We are going to know a new freedom and a new happiness. We will not regret the past or wish to shut the door on it.

We will comprehend the word *serenity*, and we will know peace. No matter how far down the scale we have gone, we will see how our experiences can benefit others. The feeling of uselessness and self-pity will disappear.

We will gain interest in our fellows. Self-seeking will slip away. Our whole attitude and outlook on life will change. Fear of people and of economic insecurity will leave us. We will intuitively know how to handle situations which used to baffle us. We will suddenly realize that our Higher Power is doing for us what we could not do for ourselves.

(Adapted from *Alcoholics Anonymous*, 4th ed., pp. 83–84)

On Recovery

We who are dually diagnosed are compelled to walk a long and narrow path. When we go out of control with our substances of choice, we become lost. If we ignore our doctors and our therapists, and misuse our medications, our path becomes very dark indeed.

In our fellowship, we band together for common good and recovery. With open-minded understanding for each other, we honestly expose our problems and our weaknesses.

The humility we show shall never mask or cover the courage it takes to admit who and what we are as, together, we find the hope and strength that make our narrow path into a wide road that leads to peace, serenity, and a meaningful life.

Therefore, working the Twelve Steps of DTR and regular attendance at DTR and other appropriate self-help groups will help us gain the rewards of sanity, serenity, and freedom from addictions.

DTR invites you to join us and continue or begin your mental, physical, and spiritual recovery.

Appendix C: Peer Support Group Resources

Alcoholics Anonymous: www.aa.org

Double Trouble in Recovery: www.doubletroublein recovery.org

Dual Diagnosis Anonymous: www.ddaoforegon.com

Dual Recovery Anonymous: www.draonline.org

Emotions Anonymous: www.emotionsanonymous.org

Narcotics Anonymous: www.na.org

Check your local phone book or look online for meetings in your area. For additional information on DTR, please visit www.hazelden.org/dtr.

Hazelden, a national nonprofit organization founded in 1949, helps people reclaim their lives from the disease of addiction. Built on decades of knowledge and experience, Hazelden offers a comprehensive approach to addiction that addresses the full range of patient, family, and professional needs, including treatment and continuing care for youth and adults, research, higher learning, public education and advocacy, and publishing.

A life of recovery is lived "one day at a time." Hazelden publications, both educational and inspirational, support and strengthen lifelong recovery. In 1954, Hazelden published *Twenty-Four Hours a Day*, the first daily meditation book for recovering alcoholics, and Hazelden continues to publish works to inspire and guide individuals in treatment and recovery, and their loved ones. Professionals who work to prevent and treat addiction also turn to Hazelden for evidence-based curricula, informational materials, and videos for use in schools, treatment programs, and correctional programs.

Through published works, Hazelden extends the reach of hope, encouragement, help, and support to individuals, families, and communities affected by addiction and related issues.

For questions about Hazelden publications,
please call **800-328-9000**
or visit us online at **hazelden.org/bookstore**.